# Dear Kalman

# Dear Kalman

Smart, Peculiar, and Outrageous Advice
for Life from Famous People to a Kid

Notes and letters compiled by
Kalman Gabriel, age 12

QUILL
William Morrow and Company, Inc.
New York

Library of Congress Cataloging-in-Publication Data

Gabriel, Kalman.
Dear Kalman : smart, peculiar, and outrageous advice for life from famous people to a kid / notes and letters compiled by Kalman Gabriel.
p. cm.
ISBN 0-688-16405-6
1. Life Miscellanea. 2. Celebrities—Correspondence. I. Title.
BD431.G135 1999
170' .44—dc21     98–52508
CIP

Printed in the United States of America

First Quill Edition 1999

1 2 3 4 5 6 7 8 9 10

BOOK DESIGN BY DEBBIE GLASSERMAN

www.williammorrow.com

To Kenny, Marsha, Adam, Jane, Frank, and Jude;

to Mary, who is an intricate part of my life;

to my grandparents Jona and Gerd.


And, most important, to my parents, Linda and Dov,

and my sister, Leah, for their love, generosity,

and creativity and without whom this book

would never have been created.

# Acknowledgments

First and foremost, I would like to thank Doris Cooper, my amazing editor at William Morrow. Her creativity and wisdom are largely responsible for what the book is today. She and her assistant, Kelli Martin, worked overtime many nights. They both deserve a hard-earned break.

Great thanks to my literary agent, Jimmy Vines, who believed in this project when no one else would. It is no wonder that his savvy and acumen have made him the top in his business.

Thanks to my father, Dov Gabriel, who was such a key element in the entire project. When I fell behind, he picked up the slack, spending hours at a time locating hard-to-find scientists and doctors. I am truly appreciative of his encouragement. Also, a warm thanks to Seymour Zuckerbrod and Kolortron Systems, Inc. for the vivid photos and complementary composites. I would like to thank the America-Israel Friendship League for allowing me to explore Israel. John Roth, my mentor and fellow sports fan, inspired me to read and write more.

I would also like to acknowledge all of my friends, who have always supported and cheered for me—even before they knew I was having a book published. I give thanks and a shout out to them all. And I acknowledge the people to whom I am perhaps most grateful: the kind and extremely generous individuals who took the time to write.

# Contents

# Introduction

**AS A TWELVE-YEAR-OLD** with a very limited allowance, I was priced out of purchasing signed basketball, hockey, and baseball cards. Yet I still wanted to find a way to collect autographs. And the more I thought about it, the more I realized that it wasn't just signatures I wanted, but rather to connect with people, to know something about those I admired beyond what I saw on television or read.

So, as a young man with a bona fide curiosity about life, I began writing an avalanche of letters. Like many people, I especially wanted to know how the successful and famous got to where they were: I wanted to know their secrets, their mantras, the rules and inspirations they lived by. I was looking for clues and guidance for myself as I began to set my own goals and think about the future.

I wrote to actors, athletes, journalists, politicians, writers, business tycoons, judges, Nobel laureates, scientists, and other experts. My question was short and direct but not simple: "If you could give me advice for life, what would it be?" I hoped to get wide-ranging and open-ended answers from the brightest minds who have helped shape our world. And answers poured in—from America's most famous and even from some who are also infamous.

My first response arrived in a small yellow envelope with the return address of 151 El Camino Drive, a popular celebrity street. I was anxious to see which star had responded. It was a handwritten letter from Alec Baldwin (coincidentally, just the day before I had seen his movie *The Shadow*). I was thrilled. It was a sign that someone actually cared to impart his advice—even to a young, faceless kid on the other side of the continent. Knowing that Alec Baldwin had read my letter and had taken the time to respond whet my appetite to write to more people. I didn't feel that I would be sending out letters into an abyss. Rather, I was inspired that other good people would write back to me. I was not disappointed.

Financing my hobby was no easy task. Luckily, my parents helped me buy envelopes, paper, and clear plastic sheets in which I could preserve my letters. I used various books at the library and *Who's Who* to find most of the addresses. However, my search was not always that easy. I received help from one resourceful guy, my dad. Together, we surfed the Internet and found the addresses for many Nobel laureates, which were not available in my books.

To my surprise, I received a flurry of letters following Alec Baldwin's response. Every day I opened my mailbox to find autographs, letters, and solicitations to join fan clubs—and also, I must admit, returned mail with incorrect addresses. While many people ignored my letters, I was amazed at how many people *did*, in fact, respond. They were powerful, influential, and famous individuals—very busy people—who took the time to answer a child's question.

In three years, I have accumulated nearly three hundred responses and several hundred autographs. The most common answer to my question was to stay in school, get a good education, and work hard. But many people also had serious advice that was less stern: They said to keep playing sports, have fun, and forget about everything else. It surprised me that esteemed people would offer seemingly frivolous advice. Many had started with nothing and had succeeded solely by their unflagging dedication and work ethic. And yet, they opted to tell me to have fun and not to worry about the future. I admired this.

**FROM MY FAMILY'S HOUSE** on Long Island, with a library, a word processor, and stamps from the U.S. postal service, I communicated with some of the world's greatest and most interesting people. Even with the increasing use of the Internet and E-mail, it is fair to conclude that regular mail is alive and well.

Practical, illuminating, and sometimes humorous advice and guidance came my way. But what's been most meaningful is the generosity of those who wrote to me. The fact that so many people responded is about much more than just giving and receiving advice. It's about reaching out and connecting with a fellow human being. More than anything, there is personal goodness imparted in the letters I received, and that makes the world seem that much smaller and friendlier, which is as meaningful as any advice I received.

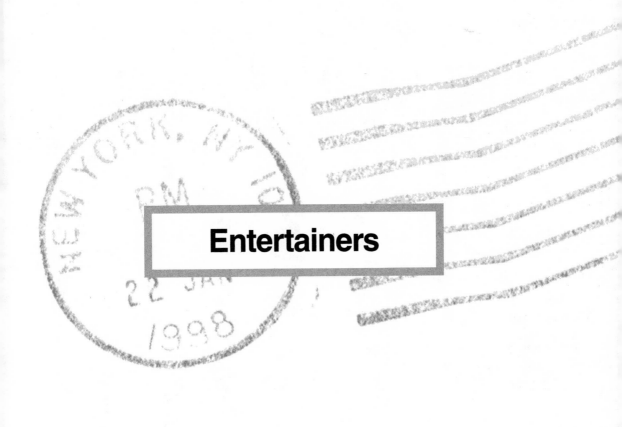

**Entertainers**

Well, my advice for life would be: don't spend a whole lot of time trying to be somebody else. Discover who you are and be yourself. You can be the best person—you can be yourself better than you can be anybody else.

—OPRAH WINFREY

Kalman —
Always try to show up.

To Kalman
John Travolta

Follow your Dream

PRODUCTIONS

NORMAN LEAR

March 7, 1996

Dear Kalman:

You might remember this every day of your life.  I try to.

"A man should have a garment with two pockets.  In the first pocket should be a piece of paper on which is written, "I am but dust and ashes."  And in the second pocket another piece of paper on which is written, "For me the world was created."

Best,

NL:gd

# MARVIN HAMLISCH

Dear Kelman:

Because you're 12, my advice is:

"Don't look for advice.

Have fun.

Enjoy!
Do the best you can in school.

Be a good son."

(You're too young for advice right now.
Try to enjoy!

Your pal,
Marvin

**INTERNATIONAL.**

1ST FLOOR   2 STEPHEN STREET   LONDON W1P 1PL   UNITED KINGDOM   TELEPHONE: +44 171 307 6243   FAX: +44 171 307 6241

26 November 1997

Dear Kalman

Thanks for your letter asking me for advice on how to proceed on writing your book.

The best advice I can possibly give you is "JUST DO IT"! *(Remember Nike?)*

Seriously, in this increasingly competitive world we live in, you have to know what you want and go after it full swing.  You have to cut through the rest of the crap and do everything you have to in order to get there.  It is simple, but there are no short cuts – it's work, hard work – it's commitment and the guts to stick to your goal, even when things get really tough.

I hope you eventually get there

Good luck

Best wishes

*Christiane Amanpour*

Christiane Amanpour

April 23, 1995

Dear Ms. Getty:

    I am a 12 year old boy from Oyster Bay, NY.  If you could give me advice for life, what would it be?

                         Sincerely,

                         Kalman Gabriel

*Try not to be official!*

Estelle Getty

July 14

Dear Kalman—

My advice is, along with "stay in school, work hard and be honest," enjoy every single moment.

Good luck!
Beatrice Arthur

December 29, 1994

Dear Mr. Anderson:

I am a 12 year old boy from Oyster Bay, NY. If you could give me advice for life, what would it be?

Sincerely,

*Kalman Gabriel*

Kalman Gabriel

Dear Kalman,

Thanks for your letter, I try not to give advice, but what has helped me in life seem to be three things
1. Find something I was good at and liked to do it.
2. Have a least one good friend who is always honest with you.
3. Follow your heart!

"STAY IN SCHOOL - GET A COLLEGE DEGREE -- TRAVEL AND UNDERSTAND HOW VAST AND DIVERSE OUR PLANET AND ITS PEOPLE ARE -- BE GOOD TO YOURSELF -- LISTEN TO YOUR PARENTS AND MENTORS, BUT ULTIMATELY USE YOUR OWN GOOD JUDGMENT."

love Gerald

STEVE ALLEN

Tenth
March
1998

Dear Kalman;

I'm sorry I've taken so long to respond to your important letter of January 25th but I simply find myself outnumbered by the avalanche of letters that hit our office premises every morning.

The fact that you've solicited advice about education demonstrates that you're interested in it, so you'll very probably make the right decisions about learning regardless of what specific suggestions I have to make. One recommendation is that you retain all of your high school and college text books. It doesn't make a great deal of sense to concentrate seriously on an issue for a year or more and then give away or sell the chief source from which the valuable information was derived.

Also building up one's own personal library inevitably pays great dividends as years pass. To facilitate that task I'm enclosing a few odds-and-ends you might consider instructive.

All good wishes to you.

Cordially,

Steve Allen

SA/jh

Enc.: "Beloved Son", "Dumbth", "How To Make A Speech", "Meeting of Minds" 1st volume and "The Public Hating".

NATALIE COLE

PHOTO CREDIT : ROCKY SCHENCK 1996

e
Elektra Entertainment

Dear Kalman –
Hold on to your dreams!
Natalie Cole

Spread the Sunshine

Drew Barrymore

Dear Kalman,

How can I, a stranger to you, advise you?

I would say <u>learn</u>. Learn all you can about the world you live in: the sciences, the languages, the arts, the people.

Treat the English language with great respect — it a a key to success. Study History — it is a key to peace.

With love,

Shelley Berman

11/14/97

March 8, 1995

Dear Kalman:

        In your letter you asked me what "advice for life"
I would give you, a twelve year old boy from Oyster Bay, New
York. Okay, here it is . . .   one for each year of your life.

1.  Never be afraid to ask anyone for advice.

2.  Listen to other person's advice, but think things out for
    yourself, because no one knows you better or has your
    best interest at heart more than you do.

3.  Be original in whatever you do in life.

4.  Never give up on any dream, unless you are absolutely
    positive there is absolutely no chance to realize it,
    and then try for it one more time.

5.  Never be discouraged or down on yourself, as long as you
    know you tried your absolute best.

6.  Failing is not a failure, only not trying is a failure.

7.  When dealing with grown ups, make your motto to not
    believe anything anyone says or promises, "until ten days
    after the check clears the bank."

8.  No idea is a bad idea, only not having an idea is bad.

9.  Always be generous with others and remember that not
    everyone has had the opportunities you have had in life.

10. Don't eat fried food.

11. Never ask a comedian or any other entertainer for advice,
    because he or she probably doesn't have any, and, if he
    or she does, it probably doesn't apply to your life.

12. When and if you should ask a comedian or an entertainer
    for advice, include a self addressed, stamped, return
    envelope, because most of them are cheap.

        I wish you a successful life, so successful that
someday a bright twelve year old asks for your advice.

January 16, 1995

Dear Mr. Cash:

I am a 12 year old boy from Oyster Bay, NY.  If you could give me advice for life, what would it be?

Sincerely,

*Kalman Gabriel*

Kalman Gabriel

*Look to the light.*

*Johnny Cash*

Kalman—

Question everything you are told by governments, corporations and religions. Question and resist!

George Carlin

MISTER ROGERS' NEIGHBORHOOD®

Family Communications, Inc.    4802 Fifth Avenue    Pittsburgh, PA 15213    (412) 687-2990    FAX (412) 687-1226

May, 1995

Dear Kalman,

Thank you for your letter.  It was interesting to know you're
looking for some advice for life, and I'm honored that you
wanted to ask me about that.

To me, what makes someone successful in life is managing a
healthy combination of wishing and doing.  Wishing doesn't
make anything happen, but it certainly can be the start of
some important happenings.  You've already learned what it
takes to be successful in life from all that you've been
doing throughout your school years, and I hope you'll feel
good enough about yourself that you'll continue to wish and
dream.  And that you'll do all you can to help the best of
your wishes come true in your life.

Best wishes from all of us here in the Neighborhood.  You are
special -- just because you're you!

Sincerely,

Fred Rogers

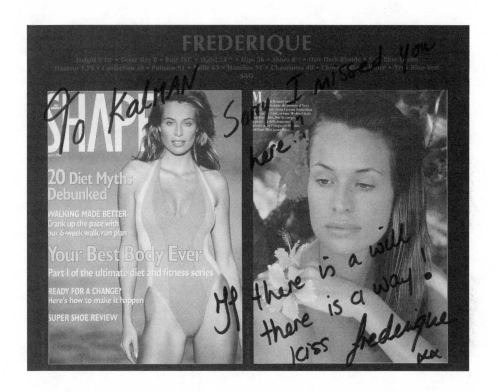

ALEC BALDWIN

July 13, 1994

Dear KALMAN –

My advice to you for life
is as follows :

1) Show thanks and pray to God
every day.

2) Live a vegetarian lifestyle.
(No beef, no pork, no poultry)

3) Work hard in school

4) Honor your mother and father.

with all best wishes –

February 21, 1995

Dear Mr. Philbin:

    I am a 12 year old boy from Oyster Bay, New York. If you could
give me advice for life, what would it be?

                            Sincerely,

                            Kalman Gabriel

*Dear Kalman —*

*Read the 10 Commandments and live by them*

*Regis Philbin*

## RICHARD CARPENTER

Dear Kalman,

In answer to your question "If you could give me advice
for life, what would it be?"  I believe a good education
is of the utmost importance, along with a determination
to do your best at whatever task you undertake. Find the
proper balance between your professional and personal life
and treat others as you would expect to be treated by them.


Sincerely,

*[signature]*

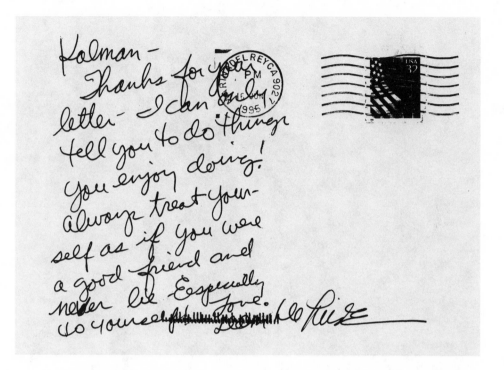

Kalman—

Thanks for your letter—I can only tell you to do things you enjoy doing! Always treat yourself as if you were a good friend and never lie. Especially to yourself.

Love,

Dom DeLuise

When you open
your heart, you
open your mind.
Danny Glover

CLARITY
SIMPLICITY
HONESTY

Sam Nein

# Andy Garcia

May 20, 1995

Dear Kalman,

Thank you for you letter of February 21, 1995.  I was quite
honored that you asked what my advice for life would be.

In response, I would have to say to study hard to prepare
yourself for the opportunities that will follow, and to
be devoted and persistent.

All the best,

ANDY GARCIA

CineSon
c/o Paradigm
10100 Santa Monica Blvd., 25th Floor
Los Angeles, CA 90067

June 14, 1997

Dear Mr. Grodin:

I am a 14 year old boy seeking advice from people whose advice is sought.  If you could give me advice for life, what would it be?

Sincerely,

*Kalman Gabriel*

Kalman Gabriel

*Help others.*
*Love,*
*Charles Grodin*

30 Rockefeller Plaza
New York, NY 10112
212 664-4602

A Division of
National Broadcasting
Company, Inc.

**Katie Couric**
TODAY

June 16, 1997

Dear Kalman,

Thank you for writing to me.  Let's see, what advice would I give to you?

The best advice I can give you is -- ***study hard***.  If you apply yourself to your school work and study hard, no door will be closed to you.

Have a wonderful summer, Kalman!

Best wishes,

*Katie Couric*

KAC/mhs

To Kalman
"a sense of
humor" is "very
important"!

Hello!
Dere!
Marty Allen

March 20, 1995

Dear Mr. Gabriel:

Thank you for your recent letter.  I pray this finds you well
and happy.

You ask what advice for life I would give you.  My advice for
you is probably the same as that given by your parents:  always do
your best, no matter what the job or how small the reward; no
matter if others are taking shortcuts or cheating.  You will then
have the satisfaction of knowing that you can rise to life's
challenges and succeed!

Please know that my thoughts and fervent prayers are with you
for great good fortune and success in all your life's endeavors.

Best wishes...and may all good things come to you always.

Blessings bountiful,

Jean Dixon

June 21 1995

Dear Kalman Gabriel
1. Get Educated
2. Be a kind and
thoughtful, and a
gentle man —
3. Get Educated
most of all —

Sincerely

Buddy Hackett

*monty hall*

June 28, 1995

Dear Kalman:

Set goals for yourself and keep working towards
them.  There are three elements to success:
First is talent.  Whatever talent you have - use
it.  Second is desire.  You have to have the
determination to keep going even when that going is
tough.  Never let anyone dissuade you.  The third
is luck.  That is the moment in life when your
talent and determination are recognized.  But
remember - you make your own luck by sticking to
your guns until that right moment.  Life isn't
always easy but remember that you are in control of
your destiny.

Good luck,

Monty Hall

MH/ca

# Kim Hunter

Dear Kalman —
 I pass to you my father's
advice to me:
 It is first of all to be,
Then to know and to do, and
only incidentally to have —
 And I add — Enjoy!
 Kim Hunter

3000 West Alameda Ave., Burbank, CA 91523 (818) 840-4444

August 17, 1995


Dear Kalman:

My philosophy is that life is full of compromise, but to compromise
principle is to give up your self-respect.  I don't want anyone
to take me for a sucker, and I don't like to see anyone else taken,
either.  A lot of things are unfair in life.  It's tough:  that's the
way it is.  But by heaven, if you can do something about it, do it!

I hope that this will help you.

Cheerfully,

David Horowitz

New Address
CBS - TV Suite 134
6121 Sunset Boulevard
Los Angeles, CA  90028

**THE RAINBOW FILM COMPANY**

Aug 10, '95

Dear Kalman Gabriel—
My advice for life is this:
① Enjoy everything as much as possible.
② Look around and explore as many things as you can.
③ Keep a diary in which you write about all the things you are feeling and seeing.
④ Don't be afraid of your feelings. Make a friend of your loneliness and let yourself know that it is all right to feel everything and anything. Don't hide from yourself.
⑤ Don't listen to any one else if they give you reasons you can't do or be something. You can absolutely do anything you want to.
⑥ Care for the feelings of others as much as you can. Try to make people feel better if you think they need it.
⑦ Don't be scared of your dreams. Make them come true.
                              Best wishes —
                              Henry Jaglom

9165 Sunset Boulevard/The Penthouse • Los Angeles, CA 90069 310/271-0202 • FAX 310/271-2753

Hi Kalman,

My advice to you
would to question
everything and ask
everyone you respect
to share with you
what they've figured
out.

Also, realize you're a
special child of God —
who created the whole
world.

Love,
Naomi

November 27, 1995

Dear Ms. Lewis:

I am a 13 year old boy from Oyster Bay, NY.  If you could
give me advice for life, what would it be?

Sincerely,

Kalman Gabriel

Study anything anyone is willing
to teach you -- languages, car repair,
cooking, anything! It will all
enhance your life.
Love
Shari

April 27, 1998

Dear Mr. Linkletter:

I am a 15 year old boy seeking advice from those whose advice
should be sought. I have received many letters of advice from
people who interest me, and come from all walks of life. I hope to
use your advice in my book. Beyond the excellent and generic "stay
in school, work hard, be honest", what advice for life would you
give me?

Sincerely,

Kalman Gabriel

Hi Kalman —
    After 85 years of living in the
most exciting, challenging nation in the
world, I have this "Key" advice for you.
    Do what you love to do!! Don't plan your
career to be rich, famous, or powerful. Select
the field you are excited about — even if that is
being a janitor or a horse-shoe-er!! Good luck!
                                        Art Linkletter

November 27, 1995

Dear Ms. Long:

    I am a 13 year old boy from Oyster Bay, NY.  If you could
give me advice for life, what would it be?

                                        Sincerely,

                                        *Kalman Gabriel*

                                        Kalman Gabriel

*Kalman,*
*Have Fun!!!*
*Shelley Long*

Kalman:
My advice.....
Question everything &
Be confident that you know best
& move to Manhattan—

Kathy.
Najimy

**From the desk of**
## BOB NEWHART

Dear Holman

Have a
dream and
follow it
as I did

Sincerely
Bob
Newhart

Advice for Life —

"ALWAYS SIT DOWN
WHENEVER YOU
CAN".!!!

         LN

Leslie Nielsen

DEAR KALMAN

ROMAN POLANSKI

Paris, December 9th, 1997

Dear Kalman Gabriel,

I'm afraid I can't be of much help.  The only advise I can give to
someone who wants to write is to... read.  Read a lot!  Good books
inspire.

Best wishes,

Roman Polanski

RP/id

Kalman,
Picture success:
leave the world no worse
than when you found it.

Love,
[signature]

**PAULA POUNDSTONE**

May 30, 1997

Dear Ms. Russo:

I am a 14 year old boy in Oyster Bay, New York.  If you could give me advice for life,
what would it be?

Sincerely,

Kalman Gabriel

Hi Kalman:

Stay in school and learn everything you can.  Education is
a wonderful thing.

Good Luck

Rene Russo

Dear Kalman

Follow your

heart!

♡

Vanna

THE WOLPER ORGANIZATION, INC.

OFFICE OF THE CHAIRMAN

May 14, 1998

Dear Kalman:

The advice I would like to give you to be successful in life is something I've always done and that is to plan ahead. I plan ahead not only days, weeks or months, but sometimes even years for things I know I want to accomplish in the future. Beyond "stay in school, work hard and be honest" add to that plan ahead.

Best regards,

David L. Wolper

DLW:jd

000 Warner Boulevard, Burbank, California 91522 • TEL: (818) 954-1707 • FAX: (818) 954-4380

Dear Kalman —
PERSEVERE!
Montell

June 14, 1997

Dear Mr. Gilliam:

I am a 14 year old boy seeking advice from people whose advice is sought.  If you could give me advice for life, what would it be?

Sincerely,

*Kalman Gabriel*

Kalman Gabriel

*Live it to the full !*

# Writers

March 1, 1998

Dear Kalman Gabriel,

I don't usually give advice to strangers. Nelson Algren, the novelist, told me when I was young never eat at a place called Mom's, never play cards with a man named Doc, and never sleep with anyone with more problems than yours. I pass that on to you, with hopes that it'll serve you as well as it has me—

All the best,

Russell Banks

The New York Times
229 WEST 43 STREET
NEW YORK, N.Y. 10036

RUSSELL BAKER

May 29, 1997

Dear Mr. Gabriel:

I am a 71-year-old man and I still do not know what advice to give myself for life.

You just work these things out for yourself.

Sincerely,

Russell Baker
(pet)

RB/pet

29th January 1998

*Dear Kalman,*

Your letter presents me with a dauntingly wide remit to advise you. I suppose a lot of people would turn down a request of such a very broad nature. I, however, see your request as imposing a bit of a challenge. At my time of life and after all my experiences, I ought to be able to give some valuable advice to young people, oughtn't I? Well, anyway, here goes:

a)      I must begin by repeating what you have evidently been told - work hard. The reasons are two-fold. First, if you work hard at your chosen subject or career, it is almost bound to pay off. Your hard work will be noticed by those above you and they will form a favourable impression, which will probably lead to your promotion. Secondly, to work hard is essential to your self-respect. To have self-respect is vitally important. Without it, you can get nowhere.

b)      At all costs, avoid getting into bad company. Once you get into bad company, *anything* can happen, and frequently far more than you deserve. The lure of bad company is a major temptation of the devil, because it is often flattering and easy.

c)      Conversely, always cultivate good company. Happy friendships are of the greatest possible value. Through them you practise give and take and they are a major source of happiness.

d)      Always do your best to stand well with important and influential people. This is not a matter of being obsequious or sycophantic. It is important that influential people should think well of you. This is a principal way of "getting on".

e)      Avoid boasting or giving sententious opinions. I well remember a friend of mine, one Denis Lock, saying to me, "Can't you understand, Adams, we don't want to know how clever you are." I remembered that.

f)      Avoid messing about in the area of sex. Pages could be written on what this means, but I will simply say that this is an area where it is fatally easy to do yourself harm.

I should think that's about enough for one go, isn't it? But if you want to write to me again, by all means do so.

*Yours sincerely*
*Richard Adams*

WIEN, September 26, 1994
SW/Tr

Dear Kalman,

Thank you very much for your letter of September 1, 1994,
and for your new year's wishes.

I am flattered that you ask my advice for your life, but
that is a very difficult thing to do in a general way.
Each human being is an individual and has to make his own
way in life - always in keeping with his character, his
talents, his upbringing, and his aspirations. I am sure
that you are well on the way to maturity and finding out
who you are as you study for your bar mitzvah. Nevertheless,
I would like to share some of my thoughts with you and my
general experience with young people of your age.

It is hard to impart to you youngsters what it was that
we experienced during the war. It is so terrible, so very
nightmarish, that it is little wonder that so many young
people tend to look away and say, it is all history and not
one of our immediate concerns. But that is where we, the
survivors, have to step in and tell them, again and again,
that all this really did happen and that it is more important
for all of you than you can even imagine. For you are used
to living in freedom, but you should recognize the danger

that lies in fast changes, that can take away your freedom
before you even realize it.  Freedom is like health, I always
tell young people; you recognize its value only once you lose
it.  Freedom is not a gift from the heavens, you have to fight
for it every day of your life.

I know it is a very heavy burden, but the future of this
world we live in lies in the hands of you and all your
friends; but it is not as hard as one would imagine to carry
this burden, because the most important task is not to
forget the past.  And then you have a chance of learning, of
drawing your lesson and avoiding all the bad things that
happened.

I have no doubts that you, Kalman, are on the right road
to learning, though I do hope that you also concern yourself
with the things that young people at your age usually do;
sometimes the memories are too much for all of us.  But as
long as we keep them in mind, we also honor all those who
were not as lucky as we, the survivors; all of us Jews are
survivors, just remember that.

Please extend my best wishes to your parents and to your
grandparents - and all the best to you for your bar mitzvah.

                              Sincerely yours,

                              Simon Wiesenthal

**United Feature Syndicate, Inc.**
200 Madison Avenue, 4th floor
New York, NY 10016
USA
Tel.: (212) 293-8500
Fax: (212) 293-8600
www.unitedmedia.com

© Lynn Johnston Productions Inc.

January 7, 1998

Dear Kalman:

My advice for life? – When you get an opportunity, SHOW UP!
Do more than is expected of you. Keep a positive attitude. Make
goals for yourself – and use mistakes as rungs on the ladder of
experience. Money is never as rewarding as personal pride.
Remember that a lie gets you into more trouble than honesty – even
when honesty is difficult to express. See every argument from the other
persons point of view. Budget your money. Enjoy sharing what you have
to spare. Trust and believe in everyone – until they prove they are
unworthy of your trust.
Arrogance is the biggest barrier to learning. Cherish your good friends,
they are your lifelines. Read good books, believe in God, welcome children
into this world. Love them, respect them, and teach them good manners,
reverence for others and faith in themselves.
Leave this earth with the knowledge that you did your best to make
it a better place. Good luck!

Sincerely,

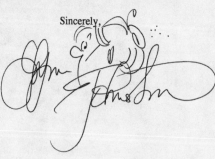

JACK ANDERSON and MICHAEL BINSTEIN
Washington Merry-Go-Round

Jan. 4, 1995

Dear Mr. Gabriel;

    Thank you for your letter of Dec. 29. My advice to you is to stay in school, study hard and always tell the truth. Never expect to get something for nothing. If you always try your hardest at whatever you choose to do, there will never be any regrets in the end, no matter if you succeed or fail.

Good luck and best wishes.

*Jack Anderson*

Jack Anderson

**JEFFREY ARCHER**

2nd March 1998

Dear Mr Gabriel,

Many thanks for your letter of 25th January.

Make no mistake, writing a book will be hard work, getting published will be even harder.  You need energy, perseverence, and of course, talent, and I wish you every success with this project and in the future.

With best wishes

Yours sincerely

Jeffrey Archer

February 18, 1995

Dear Mr. Bradbury:

    I am a 12 year old boy from Oyster Bay, New York. If you could give me advice for life, what would it be?

              Sincerely,

              *Kalman Leo Gabriel*

              Kalman Gabriel

DEAR KALMAN:
FALL IN LOVE WITH <u>SOMETHING</u>
AND DO IT ALL OF YOUR LIFE,
AS <u>I</u> DID WITH WRITING!!
THAT WAY LIES HAPPINESS!
GOOD LUCK! Ray Bradbury
2/24/95

**DATE REC'D**

MAY 30 1997

ORIG. TO: ——————
C.C.TO: ——————

May 27, 1997

Dear Mr. Spence:

I am a 14 year old boy in Oyster Bay, New York. If you can give me
advice for life, what would it be?

Sincerely,

*Kalman Gabriel*

Kalman Gabriel

*Kalman
Follow your Heart !
Do iT !   Luv,*

Dear Kalman,

Dare to be true to yourself!

Work...Peggy Lee says success is loving your work.

Learn how to type. You'll never be sorry.

Study history and English literature and art.  Science and math
if you are good at it, but don't forget the first three. They
are very important to your ethical and cultural background.

Be kind, be nice, be generous.  You
will get the benefit back from it.

I admire you for writing to me.

Good luck.  Sincerely,

*Liz Smith*

From: Dame Barbara Cartland, D.b.E., D.St.J.

CAMFIELD PLACE,
HATFIELD,
HERTFORDSHIRE.
AL9 6JE

24th January 1995.

My Dear Kalman,

Thank you very much for your
letter.

The advice I would give to you
is as follows:

"Behave like a Gentleman and always
keep your word.

Always write a letter of thanks
to everybody who has done a kindness for
you. It is very much appreciated by people.

Be honest to yourself and to
everybody else.

Always be respectful to older people
and helpful to them if you can.

Try to give out love which is in
very, very short supply in the world."

I do hope that this advice will
be of help to you.

One more thing, I think you should
always try to work hard at whatever you
are doing.

I send you my best wishes for
the future.

11/15/97

Dear Kalman—

If I were to offer any advice to you about life in general, I would say first of all, decide what your priorities are. In other words, what matters the most to you, and then act accordingly. In my case, my priorities are 1) My family 2) My religion, and 3) My job.

The other advice I would give is to give you ten important two-letter words: "IF IT IS TO BE, IT IS UP TO ME". In other words, if you want to make something of your life, you are the one who has to make it happen.

I hope this is of some help to you.

Best wishes,

BRIAN CRANE

2-98

Dear Kalman,

Advice?

Look over the next hill,
See what's over the horizon
Never let your life pass
without an adventure
from time to time.

And remember, if it ain't
fun, it ain't worth doing.

Cheers,

Clive Cussler

DOMINICK DUNNE

March 1, 1995

Dear Kalman Gabriel,

First of all, you should know I think that's
a very impressive letter for a 12 year old
boy.  Secondly, you should know that Dominick
is a man's name, so I am addressed as "Mr.
Dunne" not "Ms. Dunne."  As for advice for
life, I will give you the advice that I give
to writers who are just starting out and that
is to keep at it, advice that I think can be
applied to anything you endeavor.  Best of
luck with it.

Very sincerely yours,

*Dominick Dunne*

*P.S. Write something every day*

# NELSON DeMILLE

March 10, 1998

Dear Mr. Gabriel,

Thank you for your letter of January 25th seeking my advice to write a book.

First, I assume you mean a novel, meaning, fiction. I'll give you the same advice I've given my children, a son, 18, and a daughter, 20, and it is this: Read, read, read.

Get a list of the classics from your library and begin reading them. Soon you will be "well read." Then, pick a style you like, pick a format, a point of view, a genre, an historical period including the present, and begin to write your own novel, keeping in mind what you've read and enjoyed.

Another piece of advice I always give young people is to stay in good physical shape. The ancient Greeks knew what they were talking about when they said that the ideal is "a sound mind in a sound body." Don't smoke, drink only in moderation when you reach the legal age, and do not do drugs. Exercise and eat right. You'll find that your state of mind is better if your body feels good.

Don't follow the crowd, but be sociable.

TV and movies, even the good ones, are no substitute for reading and thinking.

Video games, computer games, and the Internet are mostly a waste of time.

And, of course, stay in school, work hard, and be honest.  But also play hard, be yourself, choose your friends carefully, enjoy your family, and learn how to say "no" when you're asked to do something you know is wrong and learn how to mean "yes" when you give your word.

Writing is a solitary endeavor, so learn how to enjoy your own company.  Don't procrastinate, don't make excuses.  Sit down to read and write, stand up to get exercise and do chores.

Above all, be aware of who you are, what you want out of life, what are your strengths and limitations, and always try to improve yourself.

And last but not least, the Golden Rule — Do unto others as you would have them do unto you.

I hope this was of some help.  Good luck.

Sincerely,

Nelson DeMille

ND:DFr

Dear Kalman,

My advice? Sheesh. That's a tall order.
How about this: Be a little kinder. Do no harm.
Assume the best about people. Be trustworthy.
The goal in life is not to have the most at
the end of it, but to have the fewest regrets.
Good luck. Jan Eliot

P.S. That's "MS." not "MR." I am one of
only a few syndicated women cartoonists. :)

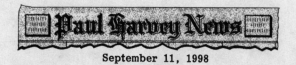

September 11, 1998

Good morning, Kalman Gabriel ...

Please use this updated quote instead:

"Get up when you fall down.  We all fall but
those who deserve a place in the sun get up
again -- and sometimes again and again --
and dust themselves off and keep on keeping
on.  The experience of successful men and
nations is determined mostly by their willingness
to get up when they fall down."

Sincerely,

PH:jw

October 28, 1997


Dear Kalman

    Thank you for your kind words about THE LOCKHORNS. It's great
to hear from a young reader who has a fine sense of humor.

    I'm flattered that you'd ask my advice for your life. I'm
not sure that a cartoonist is the best person to ask, but I'll try.

    As a 15-year-old who is writing a book, you sound mature and
focused already. So my advice is for you to get the best education
possible in many varied areas; English, Math, Science, Philosophy,
Art, Music, etc. so you have something to write about, and a
considered point of view that's credible. And, of course, keep
your sense of humor. Life and books are pretty dull without one.

    Please keep in touch and let me know how you're doing.

                    All the best,

                    Bunny Hoest

                    Bunny Hoest

Robert Campbell

18 Sep 1997

Dear Mr. Gabriel:

Advice--

1.  Try to figure out why you're writing everyone for advice
and what you can learn about yourself from that.  Then
probably stop--as you've already learned, you'll get mostly
generic pap.
2.  Strike money from your goals.  If you've got a
letterhead at 15 and live in OB you'll get sufficient
education and opportunity to have enough.  There's no virtue
in having more than enough.
3.  Pursue your interests, rather than plan your career.
It's the best single piece of advice I can give.
4.  Read a couple of hours every day.  Take the time from TV
and the Internet.
5.  Don't try to work creatively more than two or three
hours max at a time.  You just start ruining what you've
already done.  Live a full life.
6.  Friendship, love and work are the sources of happiness
(OK more pap).

                    Best of luck,

11·11·97

Kalman —

Advice for life?

Ask nothing of Anyone. Be entirely self-reliant. But be willing to give all that you possibly can to family and friends. Be happy in the face of disappointment and hardship, because happiness is a choice. If you choose to love life and be happy, and if you work hard, and if you are generous — life will be good to you. And never arm-wrestle a gorilla.

Dean Koontz

# Staten Island Advance

950 FINGERBOARD ROAD • STATEN ISLAND, NEW YORK 10305 • TEL (718) 981-1234

January 30, 1998

Dear Mr. Gabriel:

I'm sorry for the long delay in responding to your question about advice about being successful in this life.

I think the truly learned people are the people who realize that there is so much more in life to learn. Too many people think they know everything, or enough to get them by. That is never enough. The people who think they have learned it all have really not learned the most important thing there is to learn -- that every day, there is something new to learn...that you can learn something from every single person you meet...and that you learn from every experience with which you involve yourself.

Don't ever, ever be too confident. Be confident that you are going to try your best -- and then try just a little harder.

When you are studying for an exam, or preparing for a business presentation, don't ever say, ''I know it all. I've got it perfect.''

Nothing is ever perfect. Everything can be refined.

Finally, remember that there are very few brand new ideas in life. It's OK to take an old idea and use it...but somehow, make it better along the way.

Good luck. And thanks for seeking out my opinion

Sincerely,

Brian J. Laline
Editor

BJL/ek

Dear Kalman,

You pose an interesting and yet, difficult question. Advice for life? I suppose for each person it's very different. I guess I can only relate to you my own story. You see, I started in the art field at a very early age, and never stopped, so I was very busy most of my life. I wanted to avoid any trouble-that makes headlines now-a-days. (Ex. Look at Pres. Clinton) I always kept my nose clean. I didn't do drugs. I didn't drink and get into fights at clubs. In fact, I didn't go to clubs unless friends of mine were performing! I used to watch some friends snort cocaine, but I never would. Soon they stopped hanging around me, which is just as well because today they're all lost. I did just what I liked to do...draw! And it brought me a lot more than any liquor bottle could bring. Once you choose your path, don't take "no" for any answer, and don't let anything deter you! I also had strong family-ties and religion which I know helps. Don't be afraid to be different!

Sincerely,
Ray Billingsley

HI KALMAN!

All the Best! --
Ray Billingsley

Edward Anhalt

5 FEB 1998

I CAN'T HELP YOU KALMAN.
I'VE BEEN FAILING TO WRITE
A BOOK ALL MY LIFE.. THAT'S
WHY I MAKE SCREENPLAYS OUT
OF OTHER PEOPLES BOOKS.
ON THE OTHER HAND YOUR LATE
NEIGHBOR TR REALLY HAD
LITTLE TO WRITE ABOUT BUT
HE DID PRETTY GOOD.
GOOD LUCK

Edward Anhalt

DEAR KALMAN...

THANK YOU FOR YOUR
LETTER.
I'M AFRAID i CAN GIVE
YOU VERY LITTLE ADVICE
ON LIFE BECAUSE i'M
STILL LEARNING ABOUT IT
MYSELF. I THINK THAT i
CAN TELL YOU THIS.
YOU'RE 15 YEARS OLD
AND YOUR LESSONS IN LIFE
WILL BE FOR YOU AND YOU
ALONE. BUT ONE THING
THAT i AM BEGINNING TO
UNDERSTAND IS THAT LIFE
HAS A GREAT DEAL TO DO
WITH 'FAITH'. NOT FAITH IN
THINGS YOU CAN FEEL
WITH YOUR HANDS, BUT

THINGS YOU FEEL
WITH YOUR HEART.
FAITH IN GOD AND FAITH
IN YOURSELF AND THOSE
YOU CARE ABOUT ARE
WHAT LIFE HAS TAUGHT
ME TO REALLY TREASURE.

SOMETIMES HAVING FAITH

IN THESE THINGS IS HARD
TO DO. BUT THAT'S WHEN
A 'LEAP OF FAITH' IS NEEDED.
LEARNING TO TAKE THOSE
LEAPS AND HAVING FAITH
IN THINGS YOU CAN'T SEE
IS HOW WE REALLY GROW
IN LIFE. AND GROWING
IS WHAT I THINK LIFE IS
ALL ABOUT.

NEVER STOP GROWING,
KALMAN AND ALWAYS
HAVE FAITH IN WHAT
YOUR HEART LEADS
YOU TO.

...YOUR FRIENDS,

ZIGGY
AND
Tom Wilson

Dear Tom Clancy,
   How would you like to be
remembered in future generations?
I am an 11 year old boy from
Oyster Bay. If you could give me
advice for life, what would it be?

                    Sincerly
                    Kalman Gabriel.

   That is easy — A GOOD DAD.

   Nothing else MATTERS —

                    Tom Clancy

**The New York Times**
229 WEST 43 STREET
NEW YORK, N.Y. 10036

ARTHUR O. SULZBERGER, JR
Publisher

September 30, 1997

Dear Mr. Gabriel,

Here's my advice: You're fifteen years old. Enjoy
it. Don't spend your time seeking advice now. The time
will come when you will be fleeing from free advice, for it
is worth what you pay for it.

All the best,

CARDINAL'S OFFICE
1011 FIRST AVENUE
NEW YORK, NY 10022

September 29, 1997

Dear Kalman,

Thank you for your letter of 15 September requesting my "advice for life".

Our Lord Himself gave us the ultimate formula for success as a person. He said:

> Love the Lord your God with your whole heart, your whole soul, your whole mind and your whole strength. Love your neighbor as yourself. [Mt. 22:37-39]

Again, this is the formula for success as a <u>person</u>, and I am sure you are much more interested in success as a person than success in any given career.

With a promise of prayers, and

Faithfully in Christ,

*John Cardinal O'Connor*

Archbishop of New York

# The Record

Malcolm A. Borg
Chairman of the Board

September 30, 1997

150 River Street
Hackensack, N.J. 07601-7172
201/646-4300
201/646-4310 Fax

Dear Kalman:

I have learned that the world is full of choices, and I now try to keep an open mind as to whether or not I am on the right or wrong path. If I think I'm going down the wrong path, I try to change it and get on the right one. If I'm not happy, I try to choose the things to do that will make me happy.

I have found that a person's name is the most important thing they own, and it's surprising how I have been able to get them to pay more attention to me or my ideas by the fact that I remember their name or other information they might have shared with me in a previous conversation. I've gone so far as to be able to recognize and acknowledge voices almost instantly in telephone conversations, and that has been quite beneficial on a number of occasions.

Always remain inquisitive. I started my career as a newspaper reporter, keeping my eyes and ears open to everything, and I continue to do so today. It's amazing how much detail one's mind can absorb. What may seem unimportant today might prove to be important tomorrow.

I hope this gives you some ideas as you continue your journey through life.

Sincerely,

Malcolm A. Borg

**Boston University**

College of Arts and Sciences
236 Bay State Road
Boston, Massachusetts 02215

Department of English
617/353-2506
Fax: 617/353-3653

February 27, 1998

Dear Kalman:

Don't take the rewards of the world—"A" and so forth—too seriously.

Best,

Robert Pinsky

**THE**

**PRESS**

**DEMOCRAT**

P.O. BOX 569-427 MENDOCINO AVENUE
SANTA ROSA, CALIFORNIA 95402

(707) 546-2020

9/9/97

Dear Mr. Gabriel,

    Life is not simple. There are decisions regarding my personal life that I may have made differently if given the gift of hindsight. I don't wish to share the details with a complete stranger, but in general, I wish I had been kinder and more honest to others and myself.

    I have enclosed a quote by the great modern dancer, Martha Graham. A friend sent it to me in a Christmas card last year. I read it daily and find it wonderfully wise and comforting.

    Enjoy your life.

Sincerely,

Chris Wells

A New York Times Company

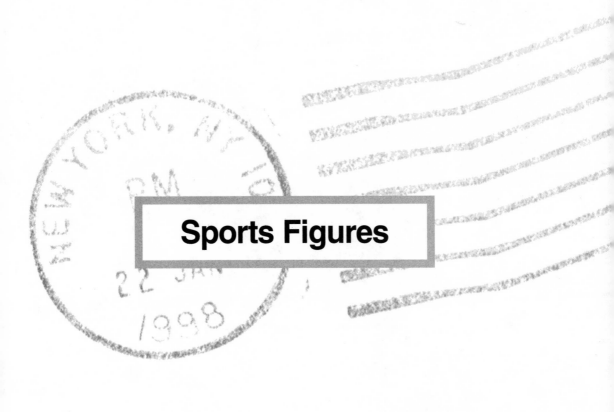

# Sports Figures

30 Rockefeller Plaza
New York, NY 10112
212 664-4444

A Division of
National Broadcasting
Company, Inc.

NBC
SPORTS

August 30th, 1994.

Dear Kalman,

Thanks for your letter.  After much thought here is my
advise for life for you:

IF AT FIRST YOU DON'T SUCCEED, TRY IT THE WAY YOUR MOTHER
TOLD YOU.

Best wishes,

Marv Albert

Phoenix Suns Plaza
201 East Jefferson Street
Phoenix, Arizona 85004
602/379-7900

Mailing Address:
P.O. Box 1369
Phoenix, Arizona 85001
FAX: 602/379-7990

June 12, 1995


Dear Kalman:

Thank you for your letter - I feel honored that you would ask for
my advice.

I've always believed that rules and regulations are important, but
that principles are what you live by.  There'd be chaos if we
didn't have rules and regulations, both in the game of life and
sports.  However, principles are what you're made of and what you
should live by:

> •Don't Lie   •Don't Cheat   •Don't Steal
> •Give Everything You Do A Good Effort

Sometimes you break the rules and have to pay the price, but don't
ever go against your principles.

I wish you much good luck and success in whatever it is you decide
to do with your life.

Sincerely,

Cotton Fitzsimmons mla

Cotton Fitzsimmons
Senior Executive Vice President

CF:mla

May 30, 1995

Dear Kalman:

Thank you for your recent letter and your interest.  My advice to you "for life" would be threefold:

- Be sure to get a good education.

- Make the most of your opportunites.

- Never settle for being average.

With best wishes,

Mario Andretti

Dear Kalman:

Thank you for your letter seeking advice for life. It is difficult to narrow down my ideas to just one or two suggestions.

However. a couple of very important pieces of advice for you to recall are, "Be true to yourself. Learn to recognize your own truth and stay focused in life. Always remember to go for it and remind yourself, 'Yes, I am the best'!"

Thank you for your interest and I wish you much success and happiness in life.

Sincerely,

Billie Jean King

Photo: John Blever

MILWAUKEE, WI 532
PM
6 JUL
1995

Old Glory

USA
Postcard Rate

## *Bonnie Blair*

500m- Gold Medal - Calgary
1000m - Bronze Medal - Calgary
500m - Gold Medal - Albertville
1000m - Gold Medal - Albertville
500m- Gold Medal - Lillehammer
1000m - Gold Medal - Lillehammer
500m- World Record Time 38:69

*I am most grateful for your*
*interest and support.  Thank you.*

Always follow your hopes
and dreams!! Bonnie

June 17, 1995

Dear Mr. Daly:

    I am a 12 year old boy from Oyster Bay, NY.  If you could give me advice for life, what would it be?

Sincerely,

Kalman Gabriel

Dear Kalman,

As you go through life find out who you are — objectivity about self. Work at being a nice person and do something about helping mankind.

*Be Happy.*
*Chris Everit*

May 28, 1997

Dear Ms. Kerrigan:

I am a 14 year old boy in Oyster Bay, New York. If you could give me advice for life, what would it be?

Sincerely,

*Kalman Gabriel*

Kalman Gabriel

*True excellence requires a worthy dream, a good idea of how to realize it, and the courage to risk failure to achieve it!*

*Nancy Kerrigan*

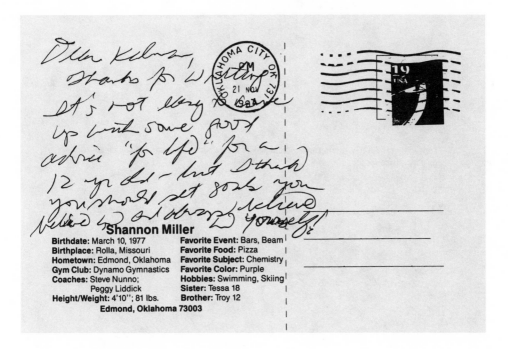

**Shannon Miller**

**Birthdate:** March 10, 1977
**Birthplace:** Rolla, Missouri
**Hometown:** Edmond, Oklahoma
**Gym Club:** Dynamo Gymnastics
**Coaches:** Steve Nunno;
Peggy Liddick
**Height/Weight:** 4'10''; 81 lbs.

**Favorite Event:** Bars, Beam
**Favorite Food:** Pizza
**Favorite Subject:** Chemistry
**Favorite Color:** Purple
**Hobbies:** Swimming, Skiing
**Sister:** Tessa 18
**Brother:** Troy 12

Edmond, Oklahoma 73003

Dear Kalman,

Thanks for writing. It's not easy to come up with some good advice "for life" for a 12 yr old—but I think you should set goals you believe in and always believe in yourself!

July 16, 1997

Dear Mr. Holmes:

I am a 14 year old boy seeking advice from people whose advice is sought.  If you could
give me advice for life, what would it be?

Sincerely,

*Kalman Gabriel*

Kalman Gabriel

LISTEN to YOUR PARENTS AND
GET A GOOD EDUCATION.

*Jay Holmes*
*Peace*
*97*

March 12, 1998

Dear Kalman,

Thank you for your recent letter. My advice to you is to just work hard and always do your best at whatever it is that you're doing and good things will happen. I hope this will be of help to you.

Sincerely,

Jeff Van Gundy
Head Coach

MADISON SQUARE GARDEN™
ITT/Cablevision

New York Knickerbockers
Two Pennsylvania Plaza
New York, NY 10121-0091
Tel 212.465.6000

National Basketball Association

**WILLIS REED**
Executive Vice President/
Basketball & General Manager

July 14, 1995

Dear Kalman:

I am in receipt of your letter of June 17, 1995. My advice to you for life is the following:

- Listen to your parents - obey their rules
- Study, be as good a student as possible. Learn all you can in life.
- Try to help others
- Find a career or profession that you enjoy and try to be the "best you can be"

Best of luck in all future endeavors.

Sincerely,

Willis Reed

WR/dm

# University of Notre Dame
## Notre Dame, Indiana 46556

*From the desk of ...*

**LOU HOLTZ**
**Head Football Coach**
**1986 - 1996**

July 28, 1997

Dear Kalman,

I can give you an awful lot of advice, but time nor space allows me to do this. The best thing I can tell you is the only thing that will change you from where you are now, to where you will be five years from now, are the books you read, the people you meet and the dreams you dream. The only person who can change you, is yourself. Nobody else can change you, but you.

Life is a matter of choices, you would be the one to choose whether you will be happy, sad, succeed or fail.

My Best Wishes,

Sincerely,

*Lou Holtz*
Lou Holtz

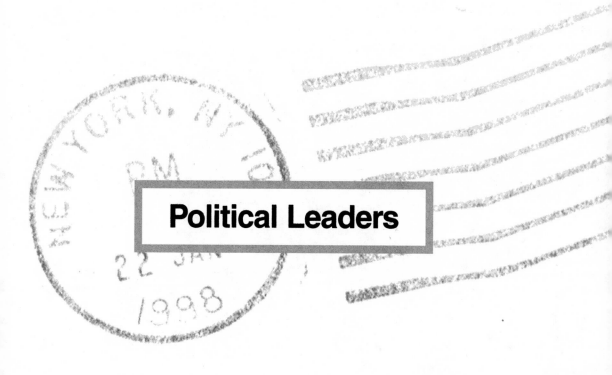

# Political Leaders

## United States Senate
### WASHINGTON, DC 20510-3301

August 10, 1995

Dear Mr. Gabriel:

Many thanks for your thoughtful note. You've brightened my day.

These are strange times here, with almost every day bringing a new challenge along with an occasional frustration. I try to remember my father's words, long ago, "Son, the Lord doesn't require you to win, He just expects you to try."

Again, my thanks. Don't hesitate to call on us <u>any</u> time if and when we can lend a hand.

Sincerely,

*Jesse Helms*

JESSE HELMS:ka

October 6, 1994

Dear Kalman:

I have your letter of October 3. The best advice I can give you is to make sure that whatever career you decide to pursue is motivated totally by your pleasure in undertaking that particular discipline. There will be those who will advise you to go into fields that are lucrative. If that is the reason, don't do it. You will spend most of your waking day at work. Regrettably, large numbers of people are unhappy every day when they go to work. They are in the wrong field, and they cannot get out. Good luck on your bar mitzvah.

All the best.

Sincerely,

Edward I. Koch

# COUDERT BROTHERS

ATTORNEYS AT LAW

NEW YORK
PARIS
WASHINGTON
LONDON
BRUSSELS
HONG KONG
SINGAPORE
SÃO PAULO
SAN FRANCISCO
BEIJING
SYDNEY
LOS ANGELES
SAN JOSE
SHANGHAI
TOKYO
MOSCOW
BANGKOK
JAKARTA

September 6, 1995

Dear Kalman:

My advice to you is this: The ideal of Democracy includes the belief that every citizen has a duty to make a constructive contribution to the Nation and the Society; therefore, give some part of your life, particularly when you are young, to your country in some form of public service.

Thank you very much for writing and for giving me a chance to share this thought. Much good luck to you in the future.

Sincerely,

Gary Hart

GH/gmcg

GERALD R. FORD

November 1, 1994

Dear Kalman:

I can't stress enough how important this period of time is in your
life. By forming good morals and learning the meaning of right
and wrong now, you are forming a pattern that will follow you
throughout life.

I encourage you to set goals and strive for excellence in all you do.
The experience, knowledge, and discipline you acquire during your
youth will be of immeasurable benefit in your adult life and how
you affect this nation and its people.

I have had the privilege of working closely with Mrs. Ford raising
funds for the Betty Ford Center for Alcohol and Drug Abuse. I have
seen first hand how alcohol and drugs can effect one's life. It is so
easy to slip into dependence, therefore I ask you not to give into
peer pressure. It's okay to say NO! Celebrate your life by being
true to yourself.

Warmest, best wishes for success and happiness now and in the
future.

Sincerely,

Gerald Ford

GEORGE BUSH

September 22, 1994

Dear Kalman:

As you look ahead to the challenges that life surely
will present, keep in mind that there is much about
which to be optimistic.  The world is ripe with
opportunity for those who work hard, get an
education, and play by the rules.

I urge you always to do your best.  Be a doer and
not a critic.  If you are fortunate enough to take
something out of the system, put something back
into it.  Give life everything you've got -- don't look
for the easy way out.  Above all else, be yourself
and have fun!

Best wishes for every future happiness.

Sincerely,

*George Bush*

## BARBARA BUSH

April 29, 1994

Dear Kalman Gabriel,

Life is full of challenges and opportunities.
Remember that one door seldom closes without
another one opening.  Each of us has gifts and talents
our communities need.  I find that by sharing myself
with others---visiting someone who is ill, helping
someone less fortunate, or simply being a friend to
one who is lonely---brings me great comfort.
Perhaps similar efforts will bring you strength and
courage.

With all good wishes,

Warmly,

Barbara Bush

# United States Senate
### WASHINGTON, DC 20510–3201

October 27, 1994

Dear Kalman:

Once again, I thank you for your letter. Unfortunately, I find myself in the middle of a hectic -- all too hectic really -- campaign schedule, which precludes me from taking on many new endeavors. So I will be brief with my advice.

Heed your parents and respect your elders. Be diligent with your studies and read -- reading is one of my favorite forms of relaxation. And always remember, nothing takes the place of hard work if you truly wish to achieve success. As Thomas Jefferson once said: "I am a great believer in luck. The harder I work, the more I have of it."

Again, my thanks. Best of luck!

Sincerely,

Daniel Patrick Moynihan

ALFONSE M. D'AMATO
NEW YORK

## United States Senate
WASHINGTON, DC 20510–3202

October 4, 1994

Dear Kalman:

Thank you for taking the time to contact me to ask for advice on life. As a U.S. Senator, the best advice I can offer a twelve year old is to listen to your parents and always be honest with them. Your parents will provide you with the most important advice anyone can offer you.

Next, I would advise you to stay in school and learn as much as you can. If you do not understand the subject matter your teachers are explaining to you do not be afraid to ask questions. Asking questions is one of the best ways to learn and remember there is no such thing as a "Dumb" question. Education is the key to your future, if you use it wisely you will be able to open many doors.

It is also important to participate in extra curricular activities, whether you are interested in sports, acting in a school play or joining student government. Such activities will provide you with a feeling of participation, commitment and a sense of accomplishment. Remember to find something that you enjoy doing and try to be the best that you can be at whatever task you choose.

Again, thank you for your letter and best of luck with everything.

Sincerely,

Alfonse D'Amato
United States Senator

AMD:js

STROM THURMOND
SOUTH CAROLINA

COMMITTEES
ARMED SERVICES, CHAIRMAN
JUDICIARY
VETERANS' AFFAIRS

PRESIDENT PRO TEMPORE
UNITED STATES SENATE

# United States Senate

WASHINGTON, DC 20510–4001

March 16, 1998

Dear Kalman:

I would like to thank you for your letter of recent date. I am always pleased when students take an active interest in government, and I commend you for wanting to learn more about public service.

My advice to those who are interested in public service begins with the values of honesty and hard work. If you stand by these principles in everything you do, you can expect great rewards. In addition to honesty and hard work, I encourage you to set high goals for yourself, especially where education is concerned. I believe that education is the golden door to opportunity, and you can never get too much education.

The greatest satisfaction that I get from my work as a United States Senator comes from helping others. I have often said that my motto is "helping others." I urge you to volunteer in your school or community to help those who may benefit in some way from your interest and willingness to help. You may be surprised to experience the good feeling you get from simply helping others.

I have enclosed additional information which may be useful to you in your studies, and I wish you much success with your pursuits.

With kindest regards and best wishes,

Sincerely,

*Strom Thurmond*

Strom Thurmond

ST/eh

**FRIENDS OF MARIO CUOMO, COMMITTEE, INC.**
845 Third Avenue, 20th Floor
New York, New York 10022
(212) 486-2850
(212) 486-3045 (fax)

June 15, 1995

Dear Kalman:

I'm very honored that you've written to me asking for advice on life. When I was a young boy, I read something by Theodore Roosevelt which inspired me and I hope it does the same for you:

> ... It is not the critic who counts, not the man who points out how the strong man stumbled, or where the doer of deeds could have done them better. The credit belongs to the man who is marred by the dust and sweat and blood; who strives valiantly; who errs and comes short again and again... who knows the great enthusiasms, the great devotions and spends himself in a worthy cause; who, at the best, knows in the end the triumph of high achievement; and who, at the worst, if he fails, at least fails while daring greatly, so that his place shall never be with those cold and timid souls who know neither victory nor defeat.
> Theodore Roosevelt

Good luck in all your future endeavors. Excelsior!

Sincerely,

Mario Cuomo

RICHARD J. DURBIN
ILLINOIS

COMMITTEE ON THE JUDICIARY

COMMITTEE ON
GOVERNMENTAL AFFAIRS

COMMITTEE ON THE BUDGET

**United States Senate**
**Washington, DC 20510–1304**
May 28, 1998

364 RUSSELL SENATE OFFICE BLDG.
WASHINGTON, DC 20510–1304
(202) 224–2152
TTY (202) 224–8180

230 SOUTH DEARBORN, 38TH FL.
CHICAGO, IL 60604
(312) 353–4952

525 SOUTH EIGHTH STREET
SPRINGFIELD, IL 62703
(217) 492–4062

SUITE 414
MERCANTILE BANK OF SOUTHERN ILLINOIS
123 SOUTH TENTH STREET
MT. VERNON, IL 62864
(618) 244–7441

Dear Kalman:

Thank you for contacting me about advice for life.  I appreciate your taking the time to write.

I believe that education is one of the most important investments to help ensure success.  Education, the great equalizer, will open many doors of opportunity to you.  I hope that it will allow you to reach real success--not measured merely in financial terms, but by the knowledge that yours is a life that has made a difference.  My schooling helped provide me with the background and tools that have helped me during my service in Congress.

Thanks again for your letter.  Good luck in school, and please feel free to keep in touch.

Sincerely,

Dick Durbin
United States Senator

RJD/pc

**Office of the Attorney General**
Washington, D.C.

July 10, 1995

Dear Kalman:

Thank you for your recent letter. I encourage you to believe in yourself and your ability to do anything you want to do, if it is the right thing to do; to always say what you believe to be right, not what you think others want to hear you say; and to do your best in every endeavor.

Best wishes.

Sincerely,

Janet Reno

**ORRIN G. HATCH**
UTAH

ROBERT L. DIBBLEE
ADMINISTRATIVE ASSISTANT

131 Russell Senate Office Building
Telephone: (202) 224–5251
TDD (202) 224–2849
E-mail: senator_hatch@hatch.senate.gov
Website: http://www.senate.gov/~hatch/

# United States Senate

WASHINGTON, DC 20510–4402

August 14, 1997

COMMITTEES:
JUDICIARY
FINANCE
INTELLIGENCE
INDIAN AFFAIRS
JOINT TAXATION

Dear Kalman:

Thank you for your letter. It is always a pleasure receiving letters from young people. I apologize for the delay in my response.

I appreciate the opportunity to share some advice for life with you. There are two specific ideas that I like to share with young people like yourself. First, get a good education. Setting and working toward strong educational goals will help you reach your full potential in life. I advise you to learn as much as you can while you are young. Be committed to your school work and enjoy every day of your educational career. Now is the perfect time for you to develop the tools you will need to be a productive part of our society. A good education gives you freedom, insight, and control.

The second piece of advice that I would like to share with you is to be constantly aware of the world around you. It is very important to be sensitive to the needs of those who may be less fortunate than you. You are surrounded by people who need your help. Take the time to look around and be conscious of others. It is also important to be aware of current issues in our society. Take an interest in the efforts of your government and let yourself be heard. Take full advantage of your American citizenship by enjoying both the freedom it offers and the responsibilities it requires.

Thank you again for your letter. Please feel free to contact me if I can be of further assistance to you.

Sincerely,

Orrin G. Hatch
United States Senator

OGH:kdz

PRINTED ON RECYCLED PAPER

KENT CONRAD
NORTH DAKOTA
202–224–2043

COMMITTEES
AGRICULTURE, NUTRITION,
AND FORESTRY
FINANCE
BUDGET
INDIAN AFFAIRS

## United States Senate
WASHINGTON, DC 20510–3403

April 30, 1998

Dear Kalman:

Thank you for your recent letter. It was good to hear from you. I am very honored you have asked me for advice on how to succeed in life. Following are a few things I have learned that I am happy to pass on to you.

First, set goals. As any accomplished businessman, teacher or athlete will tell you, setting goals for yourself is an important part of being successful. Whether your goal is to get an "A" on your math homework, to play on the baseball team, or to someday be a senator, writing down your goals -- and then taking steps to achieve them -- will give you direction and help you succeed.

Second, work hard. Once you have set your goals, it's very important for you to work hard to achieve them. Showing ambition, being determined and focused, and striving for success are excellent ways to meet your goals and beat any challenges that come your way. Looking back on my school years, while often times I dreaded the homework, I realize that some of my toughest teachers helped me the most.

Third, get involved. When I was your age I enjoyed many extracurricular activities and joined numerous organizations -- and I am still involved in many today. Participating in extracurricular activities helps teach you skills that you might not learn in the classroom. Two of the activities I was involved with were student government and athletics. Both gave me skills in leadership and teamwork that still help me in my career today.

I hope this information is useful to you. I wish you the best of luck for the future.

Sincerely,

KENT CONRAD
United States Senate

KC:wdc3

**FLORIDA ATLANTIC UNIVERSITY**
P.O. BOX 3091
BOCA RATON, FLORIDA 33431-0991

**DEPARTMENT OF POLITICAL SCIENCE**
(407) 367-3210
FAX: (407) 367-2744

March 24, 1995

Dear Kalman:

    If I had one piece of advice for you and your fellow students
these days, it would be to get actively involved in your community,
take politics seriously, get involved in political campaigns at
an early age, and think seriously about a career in public service.

    Too many people, including people in the media, are making
public service something that people think they should avoid. Nothing
could be farther from the truth. We need our best young people
in politics and public service, and I believe the post-Cold War
era will be an exciting and rewarding one for you.

    I hope these comments are helpful.

    All the best.

Sincerely,

Michael S. Dukakis

Boca Raton • Fort Lauderdale • Davie • Palm Beach Gardens • Fort Pierce
A Member of the State University System of Florida
*An Affirmative Action/Equal Opportunity Institution*

POLITICAL LEADERS    121

# Geraldine A. Ferraro

June 20, 1997

Dear Kalman,

    The best advice I can give you is that
which my mother gave to me when I was your
age:  "Get a good education."

                    Very truly yours,

                    *[signature]*

                    Geraldine A. Ferraro

218 Lafayette Street   •   New York, N.Y. 10012   •   212-226-2965

# *Issues '96*

July 10, 1995

Dear Kalman:

Thank you for your recent letter. I always enjoy hearing from young people and learning about what is going on in their lives.

I encourage you to follow your dreams and strive hard to reach your goals. My only advice is that you always stay true to your principles, your family, and --above all -- your faith.

Again, thanks for writing.

Sincerely,

Dan Quayle

DQ:js

11711 North Pennsylvania Street • Suite 100 • Carmel, Indiana 46032
(317) 580-8300 • Fax (317) 580-8313

Paid for by Issues '96 - A Multicandidate Political Action Committee (PAC)

PATRICK J. BUCHANAN                    Feb 25/95

Dear Kalman:
    My advice would be: Don't go along with The
crowd. Be your own man.
        Best,
                    Pat Buchanan

JOHN McCAIN
ARIZONA

COMMITTEE ON ARMED SERVICES
COMMITTEE ON COMMERCE, SCIENCE,
AND TRANSPORTATION
COMMITTEE ON GOVERNMENTAL AFFAIRS
COMMITTEE ON INDIAN AFFAIRS

241 RUSSELL SENATE OFFICE BUILDING
WASHINGTON, DC 20510-0303
(202) 224-2235

1839 SOUTH ALMA SCHOOL ROAD
SUITE 375
MESA, AZ 85210
(602) 491-4300

2400 EAST ARIZONA
BILTMORE CIRCLE
SUITE 1150
PHOENIX, AZ 85016
(602) 952-2410

450 WEST PASEO REDONDO
SUITE 200
TUCSON, AZ 85701
(520) 670-6334

TELEPHONE FOR HEARING IMPAIRED
(202) 224-7132
(602) 952-0170

# United States Senate

September 24, 1997

Dear Kalman:

Thank you for contacting me.  I always enjoy hearing from young people who are interested in our government and becoming involved with the legislation which affects our nation.

As far as advice, I would say to choose the field of study that interests you most rather than making a career choice based on the issues priorities of today.  Also, I urge you to become involved in your area and local government, such as the student council or the Oyster Bay city council.  State and federal internships are other options to get involved in and to observe how the legislative process works.  Any of these opportunities would not only allow you to gain experience, but expose you to the outside world and allow you to apply what you have learned at school.

Again, thank you for writing to me.  With best wishes in all your future endeavors,

Sincerely,

John McCain
United States Senator

JM/ar

## Max Cleland
*United States Senator*
*Washington, D.C. 20510-1005*

April 9, 1998

Dear Kalman:

I am pleased to respond to your request for words that have inspired me throughout my life. My favorite prayer is the ***Soldier's Prayer*** which I am sending under separate cover. If you live your life according to this prayer, you will know much contentment.

Good luck to you in your future endeavors.

Most respectfully,

Max Cleland
United States Senator

FRANK R. LAUTENBERG
NEW JERSEY

March 27, 1998

Dear Kalman:

Thank you for writing to me.  I always enjoy receiving letters from young people like you.

To be successful, I encourage you to always try your best.  Whether you ultimately succeed or fail is not as important as what you learn along the way.  I find that my best learning experiences often come from the mistakes that I make.

While you will undoubtedly face many challenges in your life, I encourage you to look at them not as obstacles or disadvantages, but as opportunities.  Indeed, you have the opportunity to play a leading role in the future of this nation.

I encourage you to follow your dreams, and to always be honest with yourself.  It is important to make decisions based on the expectations you have for yourself, not what others expect of you.

Once again, thank you for writing.

Sincerely,

*Frank R. Lautenberg*

Not printed at government expense.

JOHN WARNER
VIRGINIA

COMMITTEES:
ARMED SERVICES
ENVIRONMENT AND PUBLIC WORKS
RULES AND ADMINISTRATION
LABOR AND HUMAN RESOURCES
SMALL BUSINESS
AGING

## United States Senate

225 RUSSELL SENATE OFFICE BUILDING
WASHINGTON, DC 20510-4901
(202) 224-2023

CONSTITUENT SERVICE OFFICES:

4900 WORLD TRADE CENTER
NORFOLK, VA 23510-1890
(757) 441-3079

MAIN STREET CENTRE II
600 EAST MAIN STREET
RICHMOND, VA 23219-3538
(804) 771-2579

235 FEDERAL BUILDING
P.O. BOX 8817
ABINGDON, VA 24210-0887
(540) 628-8158

1003 FIRST UNION BANK BUILDING
213 SOUTH JEFFERSON STREET
ROANOKE, VA 24011-1714
(540) 857-2676

March 23, 1998

Dear Mr. Gabriel,

Thank you for requesting my input in your book. It is truly an honor that I am held in such high regards.

The time I spent in the military had a tremendous impact on my life and I owe much of my success to it. The experiences and lessons learned from serving in the United States Navy during World War II and the United States Marines during the Korean Conflict have taught me the remarkable value of liberty and freedom; merits that Americans should never take for granted.

I approach all of life's challenges with my father's advice foremost in mind. He borrowed words from William Shakespeare and reminded my brother Charles and I to always 'Be true to thine self.' I value the guidance offered by my father and cherish the principles that my parents instilled in me.

Thank you for your interest and inquiry. I wish you the best of luck with your book and all future endeavors.

With kind regards, I am

Sincerely,

*John Warner*

John Warner

JW/vjc

THE SECRETARY OF THE INTERIOR

WASHINGTON

MAY 1 6 1995

Dear Kalman:

Thank you for your letter of December 30, 1994. I always enjoy hearing from young people like you because you are the adults of tomorrow -- the future of this great Nation. Your question is one young people have been asking for years. I wish there was just one simple answer to pass along to you, but there are many.

First, I think believing in yourself is the cornerstone to success. Second, you must respect the rights of others. Third, you must care for your surroundings by protecting our natural resources. Fourth, you must know your history to plan and decide where you want to go and what you want to be. Finally, be the best that you can be -- never allow anyone to tell you what you cannot become. We live in a great country with wonderful success stories about people from all walks of life who have made great contributions to this country.

I encourage young people to get involved with their communities. There are projects you can do starting with your own backyard, neighborhood, school, church, park, river front, or even a nature trail. You, your family, friends, schoolmates, and others within your community·can  start with a cleanup campaign or a recycling project. Check with your school, your local government or community activist groups to see if there exists a program you can join or maybe even start.

Thank you again for this chance to pass along a few of my thoughts. I wish you much success in your life and hope these few words have answered your question. Best regards.

Sincerely,

Bruce Babbitt

RICHARD G. LUGAR
INDIANA

306 HART SENATE OFFICE BUILDING
WASHINGTON, DC 20510
202–224–4814

COMMITTEES:
AGRICULTURE, NUTRITION, AND FORESTRY
CHAIRMAN
FOREIGN RELATIONS
SELECT COMMITTEE
ON INTELLIGENCE

# United States Senate

WASHINGTON, DC 20510–1401

November 30, 1995

Dear Kalman:

   Thank you for your recent letter asking for my advice.  I am always pleased when students take the time to write.

   One of the most important responsibilities of citizens of the United States is to vote in local, state, and federal elections.  You are never too young to educate yourself in preparation for this most important privilege, right and obligation.  If this duty is shirked because of apathy or ignorance, the voting process becomes meaningless.

   In my opinion, the best preparation for voting is to become a strong student and a skilled researcher in junior high school, high school, and college.  The mental discipline and ability to analyze information developed in these pursuits are imperative in any important decision-making process.  By developing an inquiring mind and using it to sift through information thoroughly, while organizing knowledge in an objective fashion, one maximizes decision-making opportunities.  An effective voter must be able to explain and defend his or her decisions clearly and convincingly and discuss with others the merits of the choices available.  Only then, can one be sure that he or she understand fully the qualifications of the candidates and the ramifications of the issues involved.

   By reading periodicals, newspapers and books on relevant topics, a concerned citizen begins to develop a personal agenda for public officials.  Then, over time, he or she should compare the candidates to this personal agenda.

   I try to read and write as often and as extensively as possible.  I believe that mastery of language is fundamental to logical thought, profound decision-making and persuasive argumentation.  Since childhood, I have been an avid reader of everything from biographies to novels to treatises on foreign policy.  Some of my favorite books when I was in junior high and high school were <u>Lord of the Flies</u> by William Golding and <u>Moby Dick</u> by Herman Melville.

PRINTED ON RECYCLED PAPER

I deeply appreciate your consulting me for my opinion.  I
hope that these thoughts will be helpful to you, and I wish you
the best with your continued studies.

                                        Sincerely,

                                        Richard G. Lugar
                                        United States Senator

RGL/maj

PAT ROBERTS
KANSAS

302 HART SENATE OFFICE BUILDING
WASHINGTON, DC 20510-1605
202-224-4774

COMMITTEES:
ARMED SERVICES
AGRICULTURE
INTELLIGENCE
ETHICS

# United States Senate

WASHINGTON, DC 20510-1605

March 26, 1998

Dear Mr. Gabriel:

Thank you for taking the time to write me. I am honored that you wish to include my words in a book of yours. The advice I have for you is from a favorite poem of mine. It's entitled "Risk Taking Is Free".

To laugh is to risk appearing the fool.
To weep is to risk appearing sentimental.
To reach out for another is to risk involvement.
To expose feelings is to risk exposing your true self.
To place your ideas, your dreams before the crowd is to risk their loss.
To love is to risk not being loved in return.
To live is to risk dying.
To hope is to risk despair.
To try is to risk failure.
But risk must be taken, because the greatest hazard in life is to risk nothing.
The person who risks nothing, does nothing and is nothing.
He may avoid suffering and sorrow but he simply cannot learn, feel,
     change, grown, love, live.
Chained by his certitudes, he is a slave;
He has forfeited freedom.
Only a person who risks is free.

I hope these words were of help to you. Best of luck in school and all your future endeavors.

With every best wish,

Sincerely,

*Pat*

Pat Roberts

PR:ad

To Kalman. Hang in there, Work hard & stay tuned!

*Oliver North*

JOHN H. CHAFEE
RHODE ISLAND

CHAIRMAN, COMMITTEE ON
ENVIRONMENT AND PUBLIC WORKS

COMMITTEE ON FINANCE

JOINT COMMITTEE
ON TAXATION

SELECT COMMITTEE
ON INTELLIGENCE

SENATE ARMS CONTROL
OBSERVER GROUP

## United States Senate
WASHINGTON, DC 20510–3902

WASHINGTON OFFICE:

WASHINGTON, DC 20510
(202) 224–2921
TDD: (202) 224–7746

PROVIDENCE OFFICE:

10 DORRANCE STREET
SUITE 221
PROVIDENCE, RI 02903
(401) 528–5294

TOLL FREE NUMBER
IN RHODE ISLAND
1–800–662–5188

INTERNET ADDRESS:
senator_chafee@chafee.senate.gov

April 21, 1998

Dear Kalman:

Thank you very much for your letter requesting advice for your book. I enjoy hearing from young people and admire the motivation and ambition that you are displaying in this project.

My advice to you, as you approach college age and the years beyond, is to have a sense of adventure. Do not be afraid to take chances in life. Use your time to explore; you may discover that it leads to an interest you would like to spend your life pursuing. Too many people worry about their career pattern, somehow figuring that there is a set path to success. Have some fun and work at an honorable pastime that you enjoy.

Again, thank you for your letter. I wish you the best of luck in this and all your future endeavors.

Sincerely,

John H. Chafee

JHC/ms

EDWARD M. KENNEDY
MASSACHUSETTS

# United States Senate

WASHINGTON, DC 20510-2101

November 7, 1994

Dear Kalman:

Thank you very much for your letter.  I am delighted to be able to respond to your inquiry, and apologize for the delay in my reply.

I have always found that being an attentive listener can be valuable in life.  When I was younger, a number of people, including my older brothers, gave me many helpful pieces of advice.  As I have entered a life of public service, my constituents have provided me with their positions on a number of issues.  Their opinions are essential in my role as a United States Senator.

I have also learned that the most lasting legacy is service to others.  I am proud to represent the people of Massachusetts in the Senate.  Helping others, be it on a team, in your studies, or in your community, is a fulfilling goal, and I encourage you to become involved in community service or school activities.  Public service can take much effort, but it can also prove rewarding in the end.

Thank you for your interest in my work in the United States Senate.  I appreciate that you took the time to write to me, and I encourage you to keep up your good work in school.

Sincerely,

Edward M. Kennedy

DANIEL K. AKAKA
HAWAII

WASHINGTON OFFICE:
720 HART SENATE OFFICE
BUILDING
WASHINGTON, DC 20510
TELEPHONE: (202) 224-6361

HONOLULU OFFICE:
3104 PRINCE JONAH KUHIO
KALANIANAOLE FEDERAL BUILDING
P.O. BOX 50144
HONOLULU, HI 96850
TELEPHONE: (808) 522-8970

**United States Senate**
WASHINGTON, DC 20510–1103

MEMBER:
COMMITTEE ON ENERGY AND
NATURAL RESOURCES
COMMITTEE ON GOVERNMENTAL AFFAIRS
COMMITTEE ON INDIAN AFFAIRS
COMMITTEE ON VETERANS' AFFAIRS

March 13, 1998

Dear Kalman:

I am writing in response to your letter requesting my advice.

As a former teacher and principal, I strongly believe that an individual's success stems from a obtaining a quality education. Being educated helps individuals pursue their goals. However, education is just one ingredient of success. To be successful, you also have to be able to stand up for what is right, not just what is popular, and you should have compassion and understanding for those less fortunate than yourself.

Success is measured in many different ways, but if you believe in yourself and what you can do to improve the things around you, you will be a well-rounded, compassionate individual.

Thank you for writing to me, and I wish you the best as you continue to pursue your future endeavors.

Aloha pumehana,

DANIEL K. AKAKA
U.S. Senator

# United States Senate

OFFICE OF THE MAJORITY LEADER

WASHINGTON, DC 20510–7010

September 5, 1997

Dear Kalman:

Thank you for your letter of August 24th seeking my advice. I enjoyed hearing from you and appreciate your taking the time to write. I am more than happy to share with you the formulas and philosophies for success which I have found to be most effective in my search for contentment both with my career as well as other aspects of my life.

To begin with, I believe it is essential for an individual to possess complete dedication to their dreams in order to have a goal towards which to strive. I have always had a clear vision of what I wanted from life; therefore, I pursued all the necessary avenues in order to get where I am today. It was not always easy, in fact, often times it was terribly difficult, but through determination, perseverance, and confidence in myself as well as my abilities, I have been able to attain my goals.

A commitment to my family, community, and country, and a devout faith in God must also be mentioned in my advice to you. These areas of my life are constant sources of support and encouragement and act as my daily foundation.

I hope these few anecdotes will be helpful to you. Again, thank you for contacting me and please let me know if I may be of further assistance. With kind regards and best wishes, I am

Sincerely yours,

Trent Lott

TL:shw

BILL ARCHER
7TH DISTRICT, TEXAS

CHAIRMAN
WAYS AND MEANS
COMMITTEE

JOINT COMMITTEE
ON TAXATION

**Congress of the United States**
**House of Representatives**

June 2, 1997

WASHINGTON OFFICE:
1236 LONGWORTH
HOUSE OFFICE BUILDING
WASHINGTON, DC 20515-4307
(202) 225-2571
FAX (202) 225-4381

DISTRICT OFFICE:
10000 MEMORIAL DRIVE, SUITE 620
HOUSTON, TX 77024-3490
(713) 682-8828
FAX (713) 680-8070

Dear Kalman:

Thank you very much for your May 30th letter.

I appreciate your letter seeking my advice concerning your life plans. There are many opportunities available to you in our society, and your future is only limited by your dreams and aspirations. I would advise you to strive for moral, spiritual, and academic excellence. Continue to work hard in school and take part in service activities in your community. It is also important to take part in our government and be an active voice in our representative democracy by staying informed about current issues and expressing your concerns to elected officials.

By writing this letter to me, I am sure that you are headed in the right direction. Good luck in the future and let me know if I could be of any further assistance.

With best regards,

Sincerely,

Bill Archer
Member of Congress

BA/mma

WENDELL H. FORD
KENTUCKY

COMMITTEES:

COMMERCE, SCIENCE,
AND TRANSPORTATION

ENERGY AND
NATURAL RESOURCES

RULES AND
ADMINISTRATION

## United States Senate
WASHINGTON, DC 20510–1701

April 3, 1998

Dear Kalman:

Thank you for your recent letter regarding your advice book.
I commend you on your initiative and tenacity.  I wish you
success in this endeavor.

Whenever I meet enterprising young people who are seeking
advice, like yourself, I always challenge them to be true to
themselves.  In today's world, there are many forces that can
sway us each from the path that is distinctively our own.  No one
else can describe that elusive path for you; you must seek it out
of your own accord.  I believe, however, that listening to your
own values and beliefs, to your own heart, will lead you the
right way.

I hope this proves helpful.  Best wishes.

Sincerely,

*Wendell Ford*

DISTRICT OFFICES:

343 WALLER AVENUE
LEXINGTON, KY 40504
(606) 233-2484

1072 NEW FEDERAL BUILDING
LOUISVILLE, KY 40202
(502) 582-6251

19 U.S. POST OFFICE AND COURTHOUSE
COVINGTON, KY 41011
(606) 491-7929

305 FEDERAL BUILDING
OWENSBORO, KY 42301
(502) 685-5158

PRINTED ON RECYCLED PAPER

# United States Senate
## WASHINGTON, DC 20510-2704

September 16, 1997

Dear Kalman:

Thank you very much for contacting my office.  I am always
pleased when I hear from young people and I am very happy to
assist you.

I have had many excellent learning experiences in my
lifetime, but the best advice I can offer is to live each day
fully and the best you can--no one knows what tomorrow will hold.
Learn from the past, but don't dwell on it.  Don't try to figure
out how you'd live your life over again.

A favorite quote of mine is the  "Sermon on the Mount" from
the Bible.  This passage provides us with excellent words by
which to live.

Once again, thank you for contacting me.  I hope you will
continue to contact me with any future questions.

Sincerely,

J. Robert Kerrey

JRK:kah

*Kalman —*

*these give in!*

*Jack Kemp*

**Jack Kemp**
1776 I Street, N.W., Suite 890
Washington, D.C. 20006
(202) 452-8200

LYNDON B. JOHNSON SCHOOL OF PUBLIC AFFAIRS

THE UNIVERSITY OF TEXAS AT AUSTIN

*Drawer Y · University Station · Austin, Texas 78713-8925 · (512) 471-4962 · FAX (512) 471-1835*

August 10, 1995

Dear Kalman:

Advice I would pass along to young people would be, "Always work to improve your mind, for no one can take that away from you." This important bit of advice I received when I was a young girl. I have applied this to my life and found that it served me well.

Best wishes to you for success in future endeavors.

Sincerely,

Barbara Jordan

**HOWELL HEFLIN**
ALABAMA

COMMITTEE ON AGRICULTURE,
NUTRITION, AND FORESTRY
COMMITTEE ON THE JUDICIARY
COMMITTEE ON SMALL BUSINESS

☐ 728 SENATE HART BUILDING
WASHINGTON, DC 20510-0101
(202) 224-4124

## United States Senate

WASHINGTON, DC 20510-0101

STATE OFFICES:

☐ 341 FEDERAL BUILDING
1800 FIFTH AVENUE NORTH
BIRMINGHAM, AL 35203
(205) 731-1500

☐ 437 U.S. COURTHOUSE
MOBILE, AL 36602
(334) 690-3167

⌐ FEDERAL COURTHOUSE, B-29
15 LEE STREET
MONTGOMERY, AL 36104
(334) 265-9507

☐ 104 WEST 5TH STREET
P.O. BOX 228
TUSCUMBIA, AL 35674
(205) 381-7060

August 11, 1995

Dear Kalman:

Thank you for writing to me. I was pleased to receive your letter. Also, I am happy to provide you with my advice for life.

My advice is to approach life as you would building a house. You need to prepare a firm foundation. This means getting a good education, staying physically fit and healthy, and setting good moral standards for yourself. This foundation is essential to achievement in life.

With these things you can begin building a life that will be successful. Education, health and morals will allow you to achieve your goals and dreams.

I hope this advice will be of benefit to you. Mistakes are to be expected throughout life, but with a good education, health, and morals your life will be fulfilling and rewarding.

Best of luck to you throughout life. With warmest wishes, I am

Sincerely yours,

Howell Heflin

HH/cw

## United States Senate

COMMITTEE ON APPROPRIATIONS
WASHINGTON, DC 20510–6025

March 26, 1998

Dear Kalman:

Thank you for your letter in which you ask my advice about doing well in life for a book that you may write.

I gather that you have previously been advised that to do well one must "stay in school, work hard, and be honest." It is interesting that as often as this advice is repeated, that more young people, and adults, do not take heed of the wisdom in this advice. If you presently know that staying in school, working hard to make good grades, and conducting yourself in all matters with honesty and integrity can make you successful, then you are well on your way to becoming a successful adult.

Self discipline is <u>very</u> important. Read the dictionary to enrich and increase your vocabulary. One of the most important words that I believe a young person should learn to make use of is the word "NO!". Do not be afraid to go against the crowd by using the word "NO!". In your reading, I would avoid much of the modern writings, which have a prurient appeal, and that contain foul-mouth words and obscene language. Instead, read the works of writers such as Emerson, Milton, and Carlyle. Read and learn all that you possibly can about history. Read the Bible and the Constitution.

I wish you every success in your endeavors. I thank you for writing to me.

With all good wishes, I am

Sincerely yours,

Robert C. Byrd

RCB:bmt

## SENATOR BOB DOLE

October 27, 1997

Dear Kalman,

Thank you for your note.

My advise to you is to set your goals. Make sure you educate yourself properly in the career path you decide to take. For example, to become an author, you should take English, composition, creative writing classes, etc... Once you decide on your courses, work hard to become the best author you can be. If you are happy and personally fulfilled in your career, becoming a functional part of your community should follow along naturally.

Good luck in your endeavor. With my best wishes.

Sincerely,

BOB DOLE

**United States Senate**
WASHINGTON, D. C. 20510

Dear Kalman,
    Sorry for the long
delay. My advice --
            Never
Iny ~~mover~~ to separate
the life you live
from the words you
speak.

                    Best,
                    Paul

THE CITY OF NEW YORK
OFFICE OF THE MAYOR
NEW YORK, N.Y. 10007

July 25, 1997

Dear Kalman:

Thank you for writing. I am always delighted to hear from concerned young people. With respect to your inquiry, I strongly believe that young people should take advantage of the many opportunities that are available to them in today's society. I believe that you should focus on your education, work hard, be optimistic and have the courage to stand up for what you believe in.

Regardless of our age, we all have the opportunity to be a leader. Five important leadership qualities are: 1) understanding your goals and being willing to take a risk, 2) having the ability to communicate your goal 3) you must be honest and consistent to win the respect of others, 4) you must reinforce the positive things that people are doing and 5) to figure out yourself -where you are going, what your philosophy is and what you are trying to accomplish.

I hope that my advice will be helpful to you.

Sincerely,

Rudolph W. Giuliani
Mayor

Georgetown Station
Post Office Box 3649
Washington, D.C. 20007
703 691 1900
FAX: 703 385 0189

December 5, 1995

Dear Kalman:

    The best advice for life I can give you is to read
my book, WILL.  It is filled with it.

Kind regards,

G. Gordon Liddy

GGL:ja

ERNEST F. HOLLINGS
SOUTH CAROLINA

OFFICES:

1835 ASSEMBLY STREET
COLUMBIA, SC 29201
803-765-6731

103 FEDERAL BUILDING
SPARTANBURG, SC 29301
864-585-3702

126 FEDERAL BUILDING
GREENVILLE, SC 29603
864-233-5366

112 CUSTOM HOUSE
200 EAST BAY STREET
CHARLESTON, SC 29401
803-727-4525

# United States Senate

125 RUSSELL OFFICE BUILDING
WASHINGTON, DC 20510-4002
202-224-6121

COMMITTEES:

COMMERCE, SCIENCE, AND
TRANSPORTATION: RANKING

APPROPRIATIONS
    COMMERCE, JUSTICE, STATE AND
        THE JUDICIARY: RANKING
    DEFENSE
    LABOR, HEALTH AND HUMAN SERVICES,
        EDUCATION
    ENERGY AND WATER DEVELOPMENT
    INTERIOR

BUDGET

DEMOCRATIC POLICY COMMITTEE

March 13, 1998

Dear Kalman:

Thank you for your recent letter. My advice for you is to be kind to others and study hard in school. Learn for the sake of doing well but most importantly, learn for the sake of learning. Read as much as you can. It is the very best habit one can acquire. Every book is a window into a new world.

Keep up the good work. If you are kind to others and always do your very best, you will alway be a success.

With kindest regards, I am

Sincerely,

Ernest F. Hollings

EFH/jek

PRINTED ON RECYCLED PAPER

**Business Leaders**

# BROADCASTING SYSTEM, INC.
## ONE CNN CENTER
### BOX 105366
#### ATLANTA, GEORGIA 30348-5366

**TED TURNER**
CHAIRMAN OF THE BOARD

**NORTH TOWER**
(404) 827-1337

```
LEAD, FOLLOW OR GET OUT OF
THE WAY!
```

*Ted Turner*

The WALT DISNEY Company, Inc.

Thomas J. Deegan
Vice President
Corporate Communications

November 24, 1997

Dear Mr. Gabriel:

Michael Eisner has asked me to send his regrets that he cannot participate in your proposed project.

As you may expect, Michael's Disney duties fully occupy his schedule. He simply has no free time to pursue the dozens of requests he receives every week, especially those requiring his personal attention such as expressions of opinion, "words of wisdom" or personal advice. These are requests he feels involve him personally and which he does not delegate.

Michael asked me to thank you for you interest and to send his best wishes for success in your project.

Sincerely,

Thomas J. Deegan

cc: Michael Eisner

TJD:gg

500 South Buena Vista Street / Burbank, California 91521 / 818-560-1572 / Fax 818-559-7203
© Disney

1/4/95

Dear Kalman,

How very flattering to have received your note. I hope these answers will be helpful.

1. Stay in school, get a college degree or some kind of training that will give you a marketable skill.

2. Don't drink and drive or get in a car with anyone who has been drinking. Stay away from drugs and cigarettes.

3. Always practice safe sex, both as a health precaution as well as to prevent an unwanted pregnancy.

4. Remember, it's your life. Every year sit down and evaluate what _you_ want to do, who _you_ want to be, and what kind of life _you_ want to live. The only expectations you should strive to live up to are your own.

5. Don't marry anyone you haven't had a close and exclusive relationship with for at least two years. Wait to have children for at least two years after the wedding. Ideally, wait to get married until you're 30.

6. Don't do anything illegal — it's not worth it.

7. Good friends (and close family ties when possible) are what will get you through any difficult periods in your life. Cultivate and treasure them.

8. You can't imagine how precious good health is until you lose it. Educate yourself about your body, nutrition, and exercise so that you can have a long, happy, and healthy life.

Good Luck! Sydney Barros

DEAR KALMAN

SAINT
•
VINCENTS

July 12, 1997

Karl P. Adler, M.D.
*President*
*Chief Executive Officer*

Dear Kalman,

**Saint Vincents**
Hospital and Medical Center

153 West 11th Street
New York, NY 10011
Telephone 212 604-7500
Fax 212 604-7533

Academic
Medical Center
of New York
Medical College

My first bit of advice to you would be to continue your education, study hard and take it seriously. Secondly, stay close to your parents or guardians, seek their advise often and honor them by your lifestyle.

Whatever your chosen path in life, keep an open mind to new ideas and creative solutions to problems. Read as much as you can on a wide range of topics, from the humanities to physics.

To the best of your ability follow the creeds of your chosen religion. Belief in a superior being strengthens us in difficult times.

Be kind to those you meet in life's journey as there is too much meanness in the world. Take people as you find them don't be influenced by others around you.

Whatever your life's work put your heart into it. Contribute back to your society by volunteering your time and contributing some portion of your earnings to charity.

If you marry, cherish your family and be gentle with your children.

As your parents age, stay close to them and help them as best you can.

And lastly, be at peace with yourself and your God.

I hope this helps, Kalman, best of luck to you always,

Very truly yours,

Karl P. Adler, M.D.
President and Chief Executive Officer

CHARITY SCIENCE SERVICE
SINCE 1849

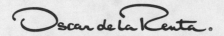

January 30, 1995

Dear Kalman:

Thank you for your letter. The challenge you pose to me in trying to give you sage advice for life is formidable, and while I don't claim to have figured out everything, I have tried always to listen much and talk little so that over the years I have come to understand certain basic truths.

The first thing I would tell you is that money does not equal happiness. Certainly, it makes life more comfortable, but material possessions can never outweigh personal dignity, compassion and loving and caring for others. People should <u>always</u> come before possessions.

Next, keep dreaming, but always temper your dreams with reality and seek out the best guidance as you choose your life's work. I strongly believe that all dreams can be fulfilled if one works hard, gives his best effort and uses good judgment.

Lastly, come to be at ease with yourself by fully recognizing and accepting your strengths and weaknesses. The more you know yourself, the more you can capitalize on those strengths and work on whatever you realize needs improvement. In this way, you will fulfill your potential as a human being.

Kalman, I am grateful for your having written to me. I have a son your age, and I have tried to give you the same advice that I would to him. I wish you much success and happiness.

Sincerely,

Oscar de la Renta

ODLR:dms

 **WILLIAMS**

**Michael T. Cohen**
President and Chief Executive Officer

**Williams Real Estate Co. Inc.**

530 Fifth Avenue
New York, New York 10036
212 704-3555
(Fax) 212 704-4404

June 16, 1997

Dear Kalman:

The following is in response to your letter of June 9th.

Don't underestimate the importance of interpersonal communication skills. Life rewards
people for their ability to "get along" with others. The economy values personality over
mere intellect or the acquisition of knowledge.

Sincerely,

Michael T. Cohen

 A Principal of
**GVA Worldwide**

Atlanta Boston Chicago Columbus Dallas Denver Detroit Houston Kansas City Los Angeles Mexico City Minneapolis Montreal New York Orlando Philadelphia Phoenix San Francisco Toronto Washington, DC Wilmington
Amsterdam Bangkok Berlin Birmingham Bristol Brussels Dublin Dusseldorf Edinburgh Frankfurt Glasgow Hamburg Hong Kong Jakarta Johannesburg Kuala Lumpur Leeds London Madrid Manchester Milan Paris Singapore Sydney Taipei

**Herbert M. Allison, Jr.**
President and
Chief Operating Officer

Merrill Lynch & Co., Inc.

World Financial Center
North Tower
New York, New York 10281-1332
212 449 7273
FAX 212 449 9573

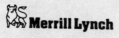

**Merrill Lynch**

July 1, 1997

Dear Kalman:

You wrote me asking what advice I would have for a 14 year old boy regarding life. Well, my advice would be as follows:

Take advantage of as much education as you can, and don't specialize too early. Get a broad education – in the humanities, history, math, science and the arts. Expose yourself to as much as possible at this stage in life, because you can always specialize later.

Learn at least one foreign language, or more if you have a talent for it. Look for opportunities to study, live and work outside the United States. By immersing yourself in an entirely different culture, you'll be better prepared for the *global* culture that will dominate the 21st century.

Finally, whether you are religious or not, adopt a few immutable ethical standards and stick to them. Things like honesty, and treating others as you would want to be treated. Be kind, and keep a sense of humor and optimism. These are qualities that will win you many friends, because they translate to every language and culture.

Thank you for writing to me, and I wish you every success in life.

Sincerely,

Herb

Enjoy it!
Then set high goals
work hard and
don't quit until
you achieve each
one.

Jenny Craig

June 9, 1997

Dear Mr. Gosin:

I am a 14 year old boy in the process of writing a book seeking
advice from those whose advice is sought. If you can give me advice
for life, what would it be?

Sincerely,

*Kalman Gabriel*

Kalman Gabriel

*Keep asking great Questions*
*Dont be afraid To be wrong*
*No one is always right*
*Think Long Term*
*Work Hard*

**HELMSLEY ENTERPRISES, INC.** _____

EXECUTIVE OFFICE
THE HELMSLEY BUILDING
230 PARK AVENUE
NEW YORK, NY 10169
(212) 679-3600

16 July 1997

Dear Kalman:

Thank you for your letter requesting advice for life.

My advice for life would be:

. Have Integrity .. Respect your fellow man  .. Dare to
  Dream  .. Work Hard  .. Persevere.

Best of luck with your book, and may your ambitions come to
fruition.

Sincerely,

Leona M. Helmsley

/hbw

John W. Martin, Jr.
Vice President-General Counsel

Ford Motor Company
The American Road
P.O. Box 1899
Dearborn, Michigan 48121-1899
Telephone: 313/323-8268

June 18, 1997

Dear Kalman:

In response to your letter of June 7, I offer the following:

- Treat all people with respect;

- Meet your commitments;

- Maintain a healthy sense of humor;

- Treasure your family and friends;

- Offer a helping hand to those in need;

- Take school, and later work, seriously, but not yourself; and finally,

- When you grow up, drive a Ford.

Very truly yours,

COLLIERS ABR, INC.
40 East 52nd Street
New York, NY 10022
Tel: (212) 758-0800
Fax: (212) 758-6190
www.colliersabr.com

*Edward A. Riguardi*
*Chairman*
*Direct Line: (212) 318-9787*

June 13, 1997

Dear Kalman:

My advise to you as a young man or later in life is to make your daily decisions based on the following:

1.  Strong religious platform
2.  Ethically
3.  Honestly, straight forward
4.  Pride in your work
5.  Treat all people kindly
6.  Be happy in everything you do, which will make you successful in everything you do.

Thank you for the opportunity and good luck.

Sincerely,

Edward A. Riguardi
Chairman

EAR:sb

Real Estate offices throughout the Americas, Europe and Asia Pacific

All information is from sources deemed reliable and is subject to errors, omissions, change of price, rental, prior sale and withdrawal without notice.

*The Company You Keep®*

**New York Life Insurance Company**
51 Madison Avenue, New York, NY 10010
212 576-4730

**Sy Sternberg, CLU**
Chairman, President and
Chief Executive Officer

September 30,. 1997

Dear Kalman:

I could write you a long essay, but my advice to you is a short list of imperatives:

(1)   Stay in school and get a good education.

(2)   Work hard - in the long run, those who work hard have the greatest success.

(3)   Treat people the way you want to be treated.

(4)   Always tell the truth.

(5)   Help others who are less fortunate.

(6)   When you raise a family, make time for your children - the time you spend with your family is more important than any material gift.

I hope I have been helpful.

Sincerely,

**NYLIFE** *for Financial Products & Services*

1211 Avenue of the Americas, 2nd Floor
New York, New York 10036-8795
Phone [212] 301•8220  Fax [212] 556•8219

**Roger Ailes**
Chairman and
Chief Executive Officer

February 10, 1998

Dear Mr. Gabriel,

I am very flattered that you are seeking my advice.  If you are passionate
and committed to your chosen profession you will probably do well.  My
advice is to love what you do in life and eventually everything else will fall
into place.

Good luck in all you do.

Sincerely,

Roger Ailes

A NEWS CORPORATION COMPANY

# Judges and Attorneys

Aspire, and work hard to achieve your aspirations.  Appreciate that, in our open society, no doors are closed to people willing to spend the hours of effort needed to make dreams come true.  And leave tracks.  Just as others have been way pavers for your good fortune, so you should aid those who will follow in your way.  Think of your children and grandchildren to come, and do your part to make society as you would want it to be for them.

Ruth Bader Ginsburg

CHAMBERS OF
JUSTICE SANDRA DAY O'CONNOR

June 2, 1997

Dear Kalman:

Thank you for your letter.  My advice to you would
be to do the best you can with <u>every</u> task you have to perform.
Make excellence a habit.

Sincerely,

*Sandra O'Connor*

Sandra Day O'Connor

LAW OFFICES

CHRISTENSEN, MILLER, FINK, JACOBS, GLASER, WEIL & SHAPIRO, LLP
2121 AVENUE OF THE STARS
EIGHTEENTH FLOOR
LOS ANGELES, CALIFORNIA 90067-5010
(310) 553-3000
FAX (310) 556-2920

DIRECT DIAL NUMBER
(310) 556-7886

SAN FRANCISCO OFFICE
650 CALIFORNIA STREET, STE. 2200
SAN FRANCISCO, CALIFORNIA 94108
TELEPHONE (415) 288-1377
FAX (415) 362-1021

February 9, 1998

Dear Kalman:

Thank you for your letter of January 27, 1998 seeking my advice for your book. I am honored to be asked and pleased to respond.

I would advise you to listen to your parents and teachers, to study hard, and to work constantly toward your dreams. Finally, I would suggest you set high goals for yourself -- but such advice to a 15-year-old collecting material for a book seems unnecessary.

I wish you the best of luck in all your endeavors.

Sincerely,

ROBERT L. SHAPIRO
of CHRISTENSEN, MILLER, FINK, JACOBS
GLASER, WEIL & SHAPIRO, LLP

RLS:bb

26059.1

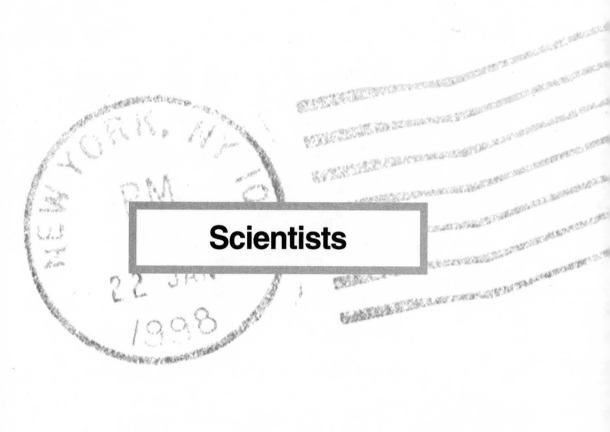

# Scientists

For Kalman
Follow your dream. Together we can make this world a better place for All life
Jane Goodall

© Mark Maglio 1990
"Fifi fishing for termites"
derived from Hugo Van Lawick 1964 Photo

**The Jane Goodall Institute**

As from Silver Spring, MD.

Dar es Salaam 5.7.98
My best advice for you would be what my mother gave to me - from age 8 onwards. (At 8 I wanted to go to Africa, then the "Dark Continent", & live with animals. Young people, especially girls, did not do that in those days. We had no money. It was end of 2nd world war. My mother said, when everyone laughed at me, "If you really want something, & work hard enough, & take advantage of opportunity, & NEVER GIVE UP you will find a way." I did. And have so - follow your dreams. And have FUN along the way. Laugh & cry & forgive & keep an open mind and
remember that you, with your life, make a difference.
Jane Goodall What sort of difference? YOU CHOSE.

August 20, 1998

D. M. Lee
## Cornell University
LABORATORY OF ATOMIC AND SOLID STATE PHYSICS
CLARK HALL · ITHACA, NEW YORK 14853

Dear Kalman,

Sorry it took me such a long time to get back to you. It is always hard to give advice since one of the main ways of learning is by making mistakes. I have certainly made my share of them.

The best thing to do is to follow your interests. Chances are the things you are interested in will be the things you are good at. Do not be discouraged if a few people are even better than you. Even though there is an enormous range of talent in the world, there is a huge number of possibilities, and you are certain to find a place where you can contribute. Every major achievement requires a high level of commitment, meaning lots of hard work, so you musn't get discouraged. In any case your work should also be fun.

But you should also learn to enjoy other things. You are young with great possibilities for growth. There are hobbies, sports, relationships with friends. These should be pursued so that you will have a whole life. Follow the good examples of teachers, parents, friends and role models. I'm not sure I've been very helpful. Best luck to you.

Sincerely yours,

David M. Lee

HARVARD UNIVERSITY

Division of Applied Sciences and Department of Physics

August 28, 1997

Dear Kalman,

    Here is my advice you requested. Set a goal for yourself, which should do no harm to any other person. Whatever your goal in life, pursue it to the best of your abilities.

Sincerely,

*N. Bloembergen*

N. Bloembergen

NB:jls

July 25, 1997

Dear Kalman:

You can get much advice from your parents and teachers. What I learned in my life was to set goals (sometimes maybe high ones) and try to stick to them over the long range. It will surprise you that if you really want to achieve something, how far you can go with determination and perseverance. Try to get the best of education you can get, work hard and believe in yourself.

Wishing you the very best for whatever career you will eventually decide upon.

With best regards,

George A. Olah

GAO:rc

UNIVERSITY OF SOUTHERN CALIFORNIA, UNIVERSITY PARK, LOS ANGELES, CALIFORNIA 90089-1661

OFFICE OF THE CHANCELLOR

January
10
1995

Dear Kalman:

In response to your request of January 1, 1995, I would say to you that as you determine your goals in life, you will have many important decisions to make.  I would urge you to define your goals in terms of the highest human values -- justice, liberty, opportunity, and brotherhood, and to practice them in your daily life.  Discipline, determination, flexibility, industry, altruism, honesty, and integrity are necessary to achieve worthy objectives.  Always strive for excellence, and turn adversities into successes.  This country has been blessed as no other with freedom and opportunity for all, but you must remember that true freedom must be accompanied by responsibility for one's self and to society.

My life and work have been guided largely by an appreciation for order and beauty in the universe, reverence for life, and compassion for suffering humanity.  The desire, instilled in me by my parents, to make a contribution to human welfare during my sojourn on earth has motivated me to do my utmost to help others preserve life and lift it to the highest level of health, happiness, and personal fulfillment.

Best wishes to you for health and a fulfilled life.

Sincerely,

Michael E. DeBakey, M. D.
2-ps

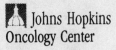

**Johns Hopkins**
**Oncology Center**

Molecular Genetics Laboratory

Bert Vogelstein, Kenneth W. Kinzler, *Directors*

October 17, 1997

Dear Mr. Gabriel,

My advice, for what it is worth, is as follows:

1) Establish high and meaningful goals for yourself. It is unlikely that you will achieve more than set out to do.

2) Believe that you can do anything and don't believe those that say otherwise. Not knowing "it can't be done" often leads to innovation and success.

3) For life in general, be considerate of others.

Sincerely,

Kenneth W. Kinzler
Associate Professor of Oncology

P.S. Stay in school, work hard and be honest.

NCI
CCC

A Comprehensive Cancer
Center Designated by the
National Cancer Institute

# SURGICAL ASSOCIATES OF TEXAS, P.A.
TEXAS HEART INSTITUTE

*Denton A. Cooley, MD*
*J. Michael Duncan, MD*
*O. Howard Frazier, MD*
*Charles H. Hallman, MD*
*Grady L. Hallman, MD*
*James J. Livesay, MD*
*David A. Ott, MD*
*George J. Reul, MD*

January 18, 1995

Dear Kalman:

Thank you for your recent letter. You asked for some advice for your future. Since you are 12 years old and will soon become a teenager, I know that many influences may affect your future direction. Let me advise you to concentrate on your school work and education. Good fortune always favors and falls upon prepared minds. I believe that you should continue your schooling and point toward a University where you can get a degree. This will ensure your future more than anything of which I know.

With best wishes to you in your efforts to succeed.

Yours truly,

*Denton Cooley*

Denton A. Cooley, M.D.

DAC:jm

POST OFFICE BOX 20345 • HOUSTON, TEXAS, USA 77225-0345 • PH: (713) 791-4900
FAX: (713) 796-2448 • TELEX: 775141 ST LUKES HOU

November 22 1997

Dear Kalman,

Thanks you for your interesting letter regarding advice for life. My advice is to work towards liberating yourself from the value systems that have been instilled into during your first 15 years, and to develop your own framework of ethics and moral behavior. You should make judgements and form opinions based on your own objective observations, and take a skeptical view of what others teach you. To be really free to make your own judgements and develop your individual identity, you should travel as much as possible, and read as much as you can, especially classics and the highest quality literature. You will need to have a grasp of human history, through intense reading, with skepticism and objective and critical analysis of what you read. Forget about TV and "best-sellers". These don't help you at all! You don't have time to spend on pop culture. To be free to live to the fullest, you will need to have a damn good job, unless you are already wealthy! This comes back to your own advice of working hard and staying in school. When you choose your career, make sure you are really passionate about what you do, otherwise you are wasting your time. You should try to be very best at what you do – only listen to the best music, read the best books, go to the best places.

Rejecting religious doctrine would be a good start. If you choose to embrace a religion later on, when you have investigated all of them thoroughly, and been to places where these religions evolved, and understood why and how they evolved, so be it. But I doubt if you will. The fact that religions are geographically balkanized just shows you how little people think for themselves and how easily they accept what is around them. Ignorance, superstition, religion, bigotry, small mindedness are all aspects of intellectual servitude. You should reject compromise and never settle for second best. Forget the "it'll do" mentality. It won't do for you!

You should also reject any political alignments you have been encumbered with through your upbringing, and make you own decisions about what is right and wrong. You don't have to be part of any existing political camp or party. You are totally free to think and do whatever you want – but to do the right thing on your own terms means understanding the system you live in real depth, and having the courage to make your own judgements and defending them regardless of what other people say. Most of them don't have their own opinions anyway. This comes back to the issue of honesty. Most people live their lives in a cloud of hypocrisy and intellectual dishonesty. This is not for you.

To summarize, my advice is to cram your head with knowledge and real-life experience, make up your own rules about how to behave, and stick to them without compromise. Good Luck!

Yours sincerely

Frank McCormick

August 21, 1997

Dear Dr. McCully:

I am a 15 year old boy seeking advice from those whose advice is sought. If given the chance, what early decisions would you have made differently. I am seeking your advice for life.

Sincerely,

Kalman Gabriel

Dear Kalman Gabriel:

If you want to enter science as a career, my advice is to study what interests you and to seek out great teachers and scientists to guide you. As Louis Pasteur said, "In scientific research, chance favors only the prepared mind."

Sincerely,

Kilmer McCully

# UNIVERSITY OF CALIFORNIA, SAN DIEGO

## UCSD

Dr. MICHAEL KARIN
DEPARTMENT OF PHARMACOLOGY
LABORATORY OF GENE REGULATION & SIGNAL TRANSDUCTION
SCHOOL OF MEDICINE

October 27, 1997

Dear Mr. Gabriel,

My advice to you is to not seek the advice from old farts like me. Just do what you think is right for you.

Sincerely yours,

Dr. Michael Karin
Professor of Pharmacology

# University Presidents

COLUMBIA UNIVERSITY
IN THE CITY OF NEW YORK

PRESIDENT'S ROOM

June 6, 1997

Dear Kalman Gabriel:

Beware of the advice offered from those whose advice is sought.

Sincerely,

George Rupp

Low Library, Room 202   Mail Code 4309   535 West 116th Street   New York NY 10027   212-854-2825   Fax 212-854-6466

October 10, 1997

Dear Mr. Gabriel:

Thank you for your inquiry. You have asked a complex question, and I wish you the very best as you seek answers from many different individuals. Here are some thoughts that I have:

Get a good education and work hard to achieve your goals. Include service to others in your life. Pursue your interests with passion, follow through, learn everything you can about the fields that interest you, and read good books, learn languages, history, mathematics, and science. The qualities of your mind and heart together, coupled with a positive attitude, will position you well for learning and for life.

Good luck with your book.

Sincerely yours,

Richard C. Levin

Richard C. Levin

RCL:baf

### DARTMOUTH COLLEGE
HANOVER · NEW HAMPSHIRE
03755

THE PRESIDENT

October 27, 1997

Dear Kalman:

I was pleased to receive your interesting letter of
October 21, seeking advice for life.

My best advice would be to live your life according to a
conception of the purpose of life. You must choose that
purpose for yourself. I believe that the purpose of life is
to search for the purpose of life.

Sincerely,

James O. Freedman

LIBERTY
UNIVERSITY

Office of the Chancellor

November 3, 1994

Dear Kalman:

I received your letter recently and am very impressed with your request. God honors our prayers when we call upon Him in childlike faith. Here are some examples of young people just like you whom God used greatly:

David was a shepherd boy used by God to deliver the Israelites from the Philistine armies. David eventually became King over Israel.

Solomon was David's son who, when he took the responsibility of being a king, asked God for wisdom to govern the nation of Israel. Because of his request, God was pleased and honored Solomon.

Joseph was sold into slavery by his brothers and, though he went through many mishaps, he became governor over all of Egypt and saved Israel from the famine.

Samuel heard the Lord call his name and was obedient to the voice of the Lord. God made him a great prophet.

Shadrach, Meshach, and Abednego were cast into a fiery furnace because they reused to bow down and worship the golden image. But guess Who met them in the furnace? It was the Lord Jesus, Himself. When they came out, they came out unharmed for He had delivered them.

Lynchburg, Virginia 24514 • 804-582-2950

Then there is JESUS. At the age of twelve, His mother found Him in the temple instructing the religious leaders and they were amazed at His knowledge--He knew the Scriptures. With David, we see boldness; with Solomon, we see wisdom; with Joseph, we see perseverance and forgiveness; with Samuel, we see obedience; with Shadrach, Meshach and Abednego, we see steadfast faith. And finally, with Jesus, we see the Living Word being expounded. All these are examples for us to follow.

My advice to you is to read and study God's Word. There is also the need for every man to receive salvation through Jesus Christ. Once we make the decision for Christ, the Bible becomes our instruction book for life. Kalman, I hope you have accepted Jesus as your Savior so that you will have your entire life to read and study His Word and then live for Him. And someday, I hope to see you at Liberty University training to be a "Young Champion for Christ."

Sincerely,

Dr. Jerry Falwell

UNIVERSITY OF CALIFORNIA

BERKELEY • DAVIS • IRVINE • LOS ANGELES • RIVERSIDE • SAN DIEGO • SAN FRANCISCO        SANTA BARBARA • SANTA CRUZ

OFFICE OF THE PRESIDENT

300 Lakeside Drive
Oakland, California 94612-3550
Phone: (510) 987-9074
Fax: (510) 987-9086
http://www.ucop.edu

October 24, 1997

Dear Kalman:

Thank you for your letter of October 16. I am not quite sure what you are asking, but I assume you would like my views on how to be successful.

Everyone has different thoughts about what it takes to become successful in the modern world. It seems to me that without a strong basic education, your potential for success today is severely handicapped. A good education will prepare you for whatever the future brings and will serve as a firm foundation throughout your life.

In my view the most effective college education is one in which students are given the opportunity to acquire some knowledge of many areas and deep experience in at least one. What is ultimately going to matter to students when their formal education is over is not the particular books they read or the specific curriculum they followed, but the cognitive skills they acquired. An in-depth knowledge of a particular subject is essential to knowing how to do something--to make a life's work. To master knowledge in one domain is also to master the grammar of learning, the intellectual skills and problem-solving discipline that can be applied to learning virtually anything. Every student who possesses this grammar has the foundation on which future learning can be built.

Although you feel that "stay in school, work hard, be honest" is generic advice, it is very sound advice nonetheless.

Sincerely,

Richard C. Atkinson
President

# CLAREMONT MCKENNA COLLEGE

*Office of the President*

June 1, 1998

Dear Kalman:

It is impossible for me to give you any specific advice in a brief letter that would not be what you have called generic. I will just suggest a book that you may find of interest, at least I found it of interest when I was about your age. Take a look at the autobiography of Benjamin Franklin.

Best of luck.

Sincerely,

Jack L. Stark

JLS:c

Bauer Center, 500 E. Ninth Street, Claremont, California 91711-6400  (909) 621-8111  Fax (909) 621-8790
Member of The Claremont Colleges

Office of the President

# Wellesley College

106 Central Street
Wellesley, Massachusetts 02181-8201
(617) 283-2243

November 24, 1997

Dear Kalman,

Thank you very much for your letter of October 27. I am honored to be included among those whose advice you believe "should be sought." To the "excellent and generic" stay in school, etc., I would add the thought that you should spend your life exploring what it is you love to do and do best and matching that great gift of yours to the great needs of this world. And by all means do write your book. Best of luck.

Sincerely,

Diana Chapman Walsh
President

DCW/ls

OFFICE OF THE PRESIDENT

PO Box 6000
Binghamton, New York 13902-6000
607-777-2131, FAX 607-777-2533

December 3, 1997

Dear Mr. Gabriel:

I am replying to the letter you wrote seeking advice.

It is important to have goals in life. The kind of goals and the degree to which they encompass worthy objectives beyond one's self will determine the difference between being self serving and serving others. This consideration is important because I believe that you should strive to serve others more than to serve yourself.

The serious pursuit of your goals requires diligence and discipline. There are many diversions available in the late $20^{th}$ century, and it is tempting to stray off track but you must stay focused. In order to resist these temptations, it is essential that you choose goals that provide joy and sense of pride as you begin to achieve them. Your achievements, no matter how small, will continue to motivate you toward broader goals.

In addition, pursuit of your goals over the long haul usually requires that you have significant mentors or others from whom you can receive guidance, counseling, and support. These individuals will also share in the joy of your accomplishments.

I hope these thoughts provide some nourishing food for reflection.

Sincerely,

Lois B. DeFleur
President

## TUFTS UNIVERSITY

Office of the President

October 3, 1997

Dear Kalman:

Thank you for your letter of September 22. While I am not sure that I can provide you any greater wisdom than what you express in your letter, perhaps the following would be helpful:

(1)      Maintain your flexibility. That is, do not become too focused too early in your life. Explore many areas so that you can have the capability to intelligently discuss a variety of subjects. Furthermore, a general preparation will assure that you can easily move from one responsibility to another in an ever more dynamic society;

(2)      Learn to think critically. Your ability to adapt in the future will depend upon your being able to listen, view, and read intelligently with the attendant capacity to analyze and synthesize information and apply it thereafter;

(3)      Always remember that integrity may be your greatest asset. When others recognize that you can be trusted, and that your word is your bond, they will respect you even if they don't always agree with you;

(4)      Treat others with dignity. Everyone is important, from the humblest to the most powerful. Always be courteous and thoughtful and appreciate that even those whose views diverge from your own have worth;

(5)      Be goal-oriented. Establish goals on an ongoing and regular basis, modifying them as circumstances demand. Goals should be lifetime, intermediate, and short term. Successful people even establish daily goals, which ultimately lead to the achievement of their long term goals;

(6)      Accept new responsibility with enthusiasm. In essence, do every job to the best of your ability, no matter how menial it might seem. Doing so will tend to enhance your reputation and develop a sense of discipline which will serve you well for a lifetime;

(7)      Have a sense of humor. All successful people tend to have a sense of the absurd about themselves. They laugh easily, and recognize that we all have foibles which can at times be very humorous. In other words, don't take yourself too seriously; and

    (8)     Recognize that love is not a nasty word.  Those who achieve do so in great part because of the efforts of many others with whom they are associated.  If you truly love those people, and demonstrate that love, they will be anxious to help you become whatever you can be.

Good luck in writing your book.  Perhaps some day I can say I corresponded with a great author.

                    Sincerely,

                    John DiBiaggio
                    President

October 28, 1997

Dear Kalman Gabriel:

I received your letter of October 16 at the Carnegie Corporation of
New York where I serve as President. My final day as President of
Brown University was September 30.

Your quest for advice for young men and women looking toward the
future from the vantage point of their early high school years
interests me and your plan to compile a book of such advice is
admirable and ambitious. I am interested because I believe that the
decision by an individual about whether to become a leader – a force
for positive change in the world – is a very conscious one and one
made early in life.

As you look ahead to higher education, refuse to get caught up in
university popularity contests, prestige-seeking, ratings and intense
peer competition. Choose institutions which you believe will
challenge you and be hospitable to your needs and then try to avoid
the stress which comes from telling your friends – and even your
parents – that you have your heart set only on one or two.

Meanwhile, leave your mark on your current school. Plan to depart having left it a better place for those who succeed you. That can be *your* contribution to American school reform. Tutor, or be a mentor, for those who may not be as academically gifted as you. When a teacher has gone far to help you develop your intellectual gifts, tell him or her because that is the greatest reward our educators can have. A great secret is that your teachers need nurturing as much as you do.

Finally, remember that accumulation of facts is not the attainment of knowledge. In a country which publishes 63,000 books a year, develops new web sites every day and seduces you with music and television of questionable quality, you are given the hard task not only of selecting what to heed but of making some useful syntheses. You are not a consumer unit but a single, unique individual with great potentiality. If you honor yourself as such, your road ahead will become clear.

Sincerely,

Vartan Gregorian

/ce

The University of Chicago  5801 Ellis Avenue • Chicago • Illinois 60637 • (773) 702-8001

*President of the University*

June 15, 1998

Dear Kalman,

　　Thank you for writing. There is not much I have to say in response to your note that is original. As an educator, a pitch for education should not surprise you. Education is the greatest guarantor for a life filled with promise and meaning, as well as the best defense against the vicissitudes of fortune. It is, as Joseph Addison once wrote, "a companion which no misfortune can depress, no crime can destroy, no enemy can alienate, [and] no despotism can enslave."

　　Beyond the above, and on a lighter note, I will say to you what I have said to my children: think and speak with care, eat and laugh with gusto, and love much and long. Begin this love with family, and if any of the preceding causes a problem, or seems impossible, think hard about why and try to improve the situation.

　　With all best wishes for your book,

Hugo F. Sonnenschein

October 21, 1997

OCT 2 6 1997

Dear Dr. Hearn:

I am a 15 year old boy seeking advice from those whose advice
should be sought. I hope to use your advice to write a book. Beyond
the excellent and generic "stay in school, work hard, be honest",
what advice for life would you give me.

Sincerely,

Kalman Gabriel

Kalman Gabriel

Kalman —

I am about to leave the country.
I do not believe that there are simple recipes
for life. Advice is best sought in the
moment from friends, family, teachers and
religious instructors. Growing in wisdom is
an achievement of a lifetime. With a name
like Gabriel, I would urge you to listen out
for the trumpets of angels!

October 29, 1997

Dear Kalman:

I am flattered that you sought my advice in your recent letter of October 20.

I've thought long and hard on the subject and find that almost anything I might say would be of the timeworn "stay in school, work hard, be honest" variety. In my relatively short time at Harvey Mudd College, however, I have seen something at work that has the potential to be life changing. Our students and faculty conduct their lives within a simple honor code as follows:

> Each member of the community is responsible for maintaining his or her integrity and the integrity of the college community in all academic matters and in all affairs concerning the community.

Sounds pretty simple, but it works. On our campus, there is no cheating, no stealing, and there is genuine respect for the opinions, rights, property, and integrity of others.

My advice then would be to develop your own personal code (you're welcome to ours if you like), work with others where possible to create a community of like minded individuals, and live to that code with the pride in knowing that you are honorable in all things.

Good luck with your book and your life. If you should have the aptitude and interest to consider becoming part of the Harvey Mudd College community when you're looking at colleges, I hope you'll be in touch. Our Web site is www.hmc.edu.

Sincerely,

Jon C. Strauss

Office of the President  301 E. Twelfth Street, Claremont, California 91711-5990
909/621-8120    Fax 909/621-8360

May 21, 1998

Dear Kalman:

Your request for advice from someone who does not know you is touching, even as it asks for too much. Abstract, generic advice can only be formulaic. Understanding a life, its hopes, fears and realities, requires knowledge of what was, what might be, and what ought to be. Knowing only your name, I can proffer nothing but vague hopes, and you have received enough of them already.

But your letter prompts me to attempt to resurrect my feelings and needs at age 15. My life has taken so many odd turns since then, that nothing I was told, no advice or pleading, really affected my world view. Your request for advice can only be turned back to you: do what you think is right and don't be afraid to act boldly.

With best wishes.

Sincerely,

Neil R. Grabois

June 13, 1997

Dear Kalman:

　　Thank you for your letter of May 28, 1997. University presidents are frequently asked to give advice, typically in the form of commencement addresses. By then, though, the graduates are already set on the road to a career or graduate school, and it is really too late to have much of an impact. So I appreciate the chance to offer advice while it may still do some good.

　　I assume that a few years from now you will be going off to college, perhaps Cornell, and quite possibly with the thought that a college degree will be the credential that will launch you on a successful career. Without diminishing the value of credentials in today's society, let me tell you about a young man who went off to college with a very different goal.

　　James Madison, born in 1751, was the principal author of the Constitution; the principal author of the Bill of Rights; the author of many of the crucial Federalist Papers, the opinion pieces which convinced several key states to ratify the Constitution; a two-term President of the United States; and a legislator of both Virginia and the U.S. who won critical debates on matters such as freedom of religion and freedom of speech.

　　How did James Madison prepare himself to take on those important roles? James Madison was a small, rather shy young man of a "weak constitution." He had tutors for his early education, learned Latin and Greek, and developed a serious interest in what was then called "moral philosophy," that is, ideas about how we should act and interact in the world. He undertook what we might call systematic reading and note-taking about matters that interested him.

　　It is fair to say that he was passionate about ideas, especially political ideas. He would frequently stay up most of the night pursuing an idea, an intellectual problem, until he had satisfied himself that he understood what was at stake, what leading thinkers had to say about it, and what opinion he should hold about it.

He went off to college with a serious desire to learn something for its own sake, not in order to gain a credential. He "tested out" of the first year at the College of New Jersey, now known as Princeton, started college as a sophomore, and then completed the remaining three years in two by working as hard as he possibly could, graduating in 1771 at the age of 20. He then did something as rare then as it is today: he asked his father if he could remain there one more year to learn more -- not to get an additional degree, but simply to pursue his studies.

There is one more thing to notice about the young James Madison. He went to college not knowing what he wanted to do with his life, and he left college the same way. Nowadays we would generally frown on such lack of direction, or, as we might be tempted to say, "lack of motivation." I still remember my uncles saying to me, when I told them I was studying Greek and Latin, "Why are you doing that? How will you get a job?" In Madison's case, it was certainly not lack of motivation to work that caused his uncertainty about a career -- he simply felt no calling yet, no pull strong enough to which to dedicate his substantial intellectual energy.

This seems to me to be a matter worthy of your thought: Will you pursue a career because it's lucrative? Because it's easy? Because it's what other people expect? Or because it's what you really want to do to fulfill your deepest self?

For many students today, credentialing has replaced learning as the reason they go to college. But a college education should be about deep, serious thinking. College should be the one time in a person's life when he or she is challenged to think rigorously about fundamental issues and to play with ideas. Students who emerge from college with their minds so trained will be ready for any career; they will be the James Madisons of the coming age.

I hope you find the advice you receive, from me and from your other respondents, to be useful, and I wish you success with your book and with your future endeavors.

Yours sincerely,

Hunter R. Rawlings III

# WESLEYAN
## U N I V E R S I T Y

Middletown, Connecticut 06459-0290
(860) 685-3500  FAX: (860) 685-3501

Douglas J. Bennet
President

November 6, 1997

Dear Mr. Gabriel:

My advice is to attend Wesleyan.

With best regards.

Sincerely,

DJB/jwm

# UNIVERSITY of PENNSYLVANIA

**Office of the President**

100 College Hall
Philadelphia, PA 19104-6380
215-898-7221

June 17, 1997

Dear Kalman:

Thank you for your letter. The book you are writing sounds like quite an ambitious undertaking. For my part, I hesitate to give proclamations of advice to anyone. Rather, let me wish you well in your efforts and suggest that you continue to work hard and aim high. You sound enterprising beyond your years.

Best of luck to you!

Sincerely,

Judith Rodin
President

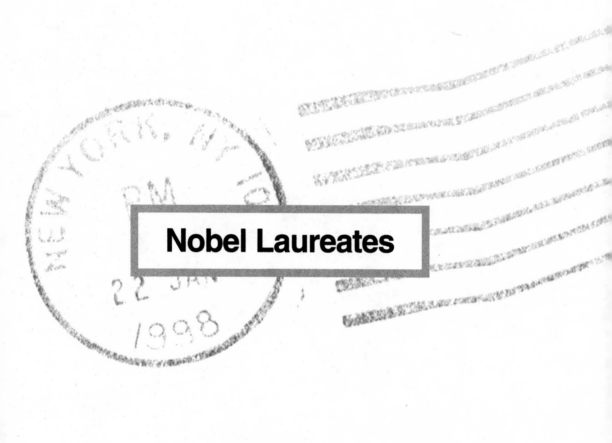

# Nobel Laureates

+LDM

MISSIONARIES OF CHARITY
54/A, A. J C. Bose Road.
Calcutta - 700016. India

Dear Kalman Gabriel,

Thank you for your letter.  God loves you.  And you
can put your love for God in a living action. For
Jesus said:Whatever you do to the least of my brethren,
you did it to me.   It is not how much we give, but
how much love we put in the giving. And love begins
at home. Pray together and you will stay together.
If you stay together you will love each other as God
loves you.  I will pray for you that you may keep close
to the love of God, and allow God to love in you and
through you.

God bless you.

*lee Teresa mc*

DOUGLAS OSHEROFF
J. G. JACKSON AND C. J. WOOD PROFESSOR OF PHYSICS

TELEPHONE    (415) 723-4228
FAX          (415) 725-6544

August 25, 1997

Dear Kalman:

Your request sounds a lot like a homework assignment, so I won't spend much time talking about my life. Suffice it to say that things have turned out pretty well, and I am not inclined to change much. However, I think I have been very lucky throughout my life.

Let me offer you some advice: You need to begin to understand who you are, what you have to offer others, and what you need to be happy and productive in return. There are so many possibilities in life, you need to find a job or profession which fits you abilities and interests. Be careful to avoid an attraction to some endeavor simply because you feel it is important. For me, I was co-editor of my high school newspaper, and for a while thought about a career in journalism. I would have been miserable! What ever you profession, you need to enjoy the doing of the work as well as its importance. Also, beware, for at some point, perhaps when you turn 40, or perhaps 50, you will look at your life and ask 'Is this the legacy I wish to leave? Does all this bring meaning and purpose to my existence?'

Good luck.

Sincerely,

Douglas D. Osheroff

# UNIVERSITY OF CALIFORNIA, BERKELEY

BERKELEY · DAVIS · IRVINE · LOS ANGELES · RIVERSIDE · SAN DIEGO · SAN FRANCISCO        SANTA BARBARA · SANTA CRUZ

WALTER A. HAAS SCHOOL OF BUSINESS

545 Student Services Building # 1900
Berkeley, California 94720-1900

September 3, 1997.

Dear Kalman:

　　The main advice I would like to give you is this. Take as many mathematics and science courses as you can, and be sure to learn at least one or two important foreign languages, and preferably more of them. This will very much help you in college as well as later in your life. What we can achieve in our lives strongly depends on how well we have used our high school years.

Sincerely yours,

John C. Harsanyi

October 16, 1997

Dear Dr. Scholes:

I am a 15 year old boy seeking advice from those whose advice is
sought. I hope to use your advice to write a book. Beyond the
excellent and generic "stay in school, work hard, be honest", what
advice would you give me.

Sincerely,

Kalman Gabriel

Dear Kalman

If you can handle it and are willing to
compete go where the best people are in your
chosen line of endeavor. They will stimulate your
thinking and they can grow along with you through
the joint interaction. Good luck.

Myron Scholes
10/30/97

**GlaxoWellcome**

Gertrude B. Elion, D.Sc.
Scientist Emeritus

August 22, 1997

Dear Kalman,

Your letter was forwarded to me while I was away on vacation. You have asked for advice for life. The best advice I can give you is the following:

Find the kind of work you would really enjoy. Then work will become "play" and you will do it with enthusiasm and be successful. Set a goal for yourself. Even if you don't reach the goal, you will have something to aim for and it will keep you on the right track.

Finally, never give up. Don't let people discourage you. When the going gets tough, remember what Admiral Farragut said, "Damn the torpedos; full speed ahead."

Best of luck to you.

Sincerely,

Gertrude B. Elion

**Glaxo Wellcome Inc.**

Five Moore Drive
PO Box 13398
Research Triangle Park
North Carolina 27709

Telephone
919 483 1664

Fax
919 315 5819

ARTHUR L. SCHAWLOW
JACKSON-WOOD PROFESSOR EMERITUS
DEPARTMENT OF PHYSICS

October 5, 1997

Dear Mr. Gabriel:

Even if I knew something about your interest and abilities,
I could hardly give more than the most general suggestions.
At your age you have a lot to learn, and if you find studies
satisfying I would urge you to learn as much as you can
about the fundamentals of whatever interests you.  That is,
if you can see any endeavor that you might want to pursue
that could provide a decent living, you might well aim in
that direction.  But do not aim too narrowly. Concentrate on
the fundamentals, and opportunities may come up that are not
quite where you were aiming but are even more attractive.

Yours sincerely,

Arthur L. Schawlow

August 22, 1997

Dear Dr. Sharpe:

I am a 15 year old boy seeking advice from those whose advice is sought. If given the chance, what early decisions would you have made differently. I am seeking your advice for life.

Sincerely,

Kalman Gabriel

Kalman:

I would have continued studying music (for recreation) and read more widely but these would have been any minor changes. Not surprisingly, I am quite content with the decisions I made and the resulting outcomes.

W. F. S—

August 22, 1997

Dear Dr. Samuelson:

I am a 15 year old boy seeking advice from those whose advice is
sought. If given the chance, what early decisions would you have
made differently. I am seeking your advice for life.

Sincerely,

Kalman Gabriel

Dear Kalman,

I have always been a quick worker, who takes shortcuts when possible. As a result, I often make small errors. If I could lead my life over a second time, I would try to be more systematic. That would be more efficient, and even faster, in the long run.

Good luck,

# MASSACHUSETTS INSTITUTE OF TECHNOLOGY

DEPARTMENT OF ECONOMICS                                CAMBRIDGE, MASSACHUSETTS 02139-4307

17 September 1997

DEar Mr. Gabriel:

I am tempted to take the easy way out and tell you that my advice is not to seek advice. What I mean is that I think it is very hard to imagine what it is like to be someone else. So even if I could think of early decisions I now wish I had made differently, that would convey very little information to someone almost 60 years younger than I am, and differently situated. To tell you the truth, I am not aware of having "made" big decisions. Things happen as the cumulation of a lot of minor events, some of which may have been decisions, usually casual.

If instead I try to think of something useful to tell you it would be this. You will spend most of your life going to work in the morning and doing a job. If the job is a drag, that will color much of your life gray. So it is very important to spend that part of your life doing something you find interesting and enjoyable. You should try to figure out what that might be, realistically, and then take the initial steps that will start you in that direction. With any luck it will work out.

So I wish you that kind of luck.

Sincerely yours,

*Robert Solow*

Robert M. Solow

**Cornell University**

Department of Chemistry
Baker Laboratory
Ithaca, New York 14853-1301 USA

Aug. 25, 1997

Dear Mr. Gabriel,

My early life was dictated by
survival; there were few options. I would
advise you not to be afraid of letting
life take you where it wants — you will
find places under your control, but I
wouldn't agonize about choices.

Cordially,

Roald Hoffmann

# GRAND HÔTEL

### STOCKHOLM – SWEDEN

For Kalman Gabriel,

"Ask Good Questions"

Nobel Week

Robert C. Merton

December 1997

| Postal adress | Street address | Telephone | Telegram | Telefax | Telex |
|---|---|---|---|---|---|
| P.O. Box 16424 | S. Blasie- | | Grand | | 19500 |
| S-103 27 STOCKHOLM | holmshamnen 8 | 08-679 35 00 | Stockholm | 08-611 86 86 | Grand S |

A member of
*The Leading Hotels of the World*

Partner
STEIGENBERGER
H · O · T · E · L · S

September 2, 1997

Dear Dr. Buchanan:

I am a 15 year old boy seeking advice from those whose advice is
sought. If given the chance, what early decisions would you have
made differently. I am seeking your advice for life.

Sincerely,

Kalman Gabriel

5 Sept 97

I would have tried, somehow, to
learn more classics, Latin and Greek
languages, and Greek mythology. I
have always felt this element missing
in my education. For autobiographical
material, see my book, Better Than Plowing
(University of Chicago Press, 1992)

**New York University**
*A private university in the public service*

**Institute for Economic Analysis**
269 Mercer Street, 2nd Floor
New York, NY 10003-6687
Telephone: (212) 998-7484
Fax: (212) 995-4165

**Wassily Leontief**
*University Professor*

September 24, 1997

Dear Kalman:

In general, once I decide to do something I gather information about it then go right ahead and do it.  Luckily, most of the decisions that I have made seemed correct.  Therefore, decide what you want to do gather all the information you need then do it.

With best wishes and good luck.

Sincerely,

Wassily Leontief

WL/mp
[Dictated by Prof. Leontief
and signed in his absence]

**FROM THE ANGLICAN ARCHBISHOP OF CAPE TOWN**

The Most Reverend Desmond M. Tutu, D.D. F.K.C.

BISHOPSCOURT CLAREMONT CAPE 7700

TELEPHONE: (021) 761-2531
FAX: (021) 761-4193

/fd

9 January 1995

Dear Kalman,

Thank you for writing to me.

My advice to you would be to believe in yourself and know
that God loves you.

God bless you.

Yours sincerely,

+Desmond Cape Town
(signed in absentia)

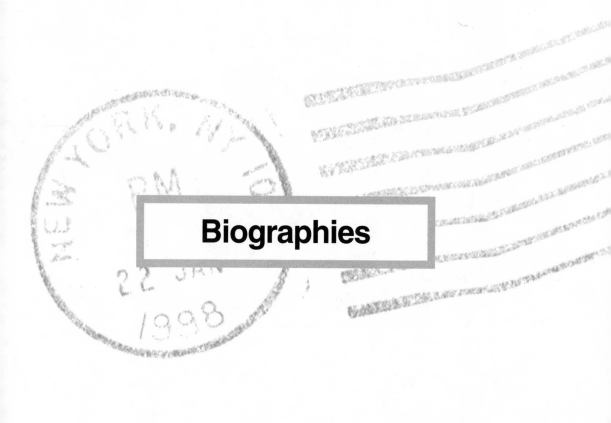

# Biographies

RICHARD ADAMS is the author of the international bestseller *Watership Down* (1972). The story follows a warren of Berkshire rabbits fleeing the destruction of their home by a land developer. Often praised as an allegory, *Watership Down* has been a staple of high school English classes since its publication.

KARL P. ADLER is the president and CEO of Saint Vincent's Hospital and Medical Center of New York. Saint Vincent's Hospital is a major tertiary care and teaching hospital in the heart of lower Manhattan.

ROGER AILES has been chairman and CEO of the Fox network since 1997. Ailes served as the president of CNBC, the financial news network, for more than two years. He left when *America's Talking*, which he started, was co-opted by NBC to be used as a platform for its new joint product with Microsoft, then tentatively called MSNBC. Ailes, a staunch Republican, was executive producer of the *Rush LimbaughShow*. Before that, he was a political and campaign adviser for former Presidents Nixon, Reagan, and Bush. (Fox News)

DANIEL K. AKAKA, a Democratic senator from Hawaii, elected in 1990, cosponsored the Employment Non-discrimination Act, which prohibits discrimination against gay men and lesbians in the workplace.

MARV ALBERT is a sportscaster and six-time recipient of the Cable Ace Play-by-Play Award, which recognizes the greatest sports broadcaster of the day. Albert's reputation was marred when he pleaded guilty to assault after a former girlfriend charged him with forcible sodomy. Prior to this incident, which resulted in his being fired, the fallen broadcasting legend was NBC's lead NBA announcer.

MARTY ALLEN is a comedic actor who was part of the famous comic duo Martin and Rossi.

STEVE ALLEN is a comedian who starred in *Great Balls of Fire!* (1989). Part wacky comedian and part erudite author (he penned *But Seriously: Steve Allen Speaks His Mind* and *Die Laughing* among others), he has hosted and produced many TV programs, written books on comedy and religion and several mystery novels, and composed countless songs. He was named to the Television Hall of Fame in 1986.

HERBERT M. ALLISON, JR., president of Merrill Lynch & Co., Inc., began his career with the company in 1971 as an associate in the investment banking division in New York and gradually rose to head it.

CHRISTIANE AMANPOUR is a CNN senior international correspondant who has worked in most of the major war zones of the 1990s, including Sarajevo, Haiti, Algeria, and Rwanda, where she covered civil unrest and political crises. Amanpour's most extensive reports have been filed from Yugoslavia; she is credited with having brought the Bosnian tragedy to the world's attention. No American network correspondent has reported as continuously from this ethnically torn region.

JACK ANDERSON is a journalist who, after twenty years of investigation, disclosed an extraordinary plot involving Fidel Castro and the Mafia. It was in his column, "Merry Go Round," that the savings and loan scandal, the Iran/Contra arms-for-hostages deal, and the danger of Saddam Hussein first appeared.

LOUIS ANDERSON is a comedic actor who starred in *Ratboy* (1986), *Coming to America* (1988), and *The Louie Show* (1996).

MARIO ANDRETTI is a race-car driver who won the Indy Car Championship in 1965, 1966, 1969, and 1984. He also won Driver of the Year in 1967, 1978, and 1984 and was named Driver of the Quarter Century in 1992.

EDWARD ANHALT is a writer who won an Oscar for Best Writing in 1951 for *Panic in the Streets* (1950).

BILL ARCHER, representing the 7th Congressional District of Texas since 1971, is known nationally as a tough fiscal conservative. He was a key player during Congress's efforts to get the 1997 balanced budget with tax relief signed into law. The 1997 budget, which is scheduled to balance by 2002, was the first balanced federal budget since 1969.

JEFFREY ARCHER is an international bestselling author of more than thirty books, including *First Among Equals* (1984), *As the Crow Flies* (1991), and *The Fourth Estate* (1996).

BEATRICE ARTHUR starred in *The Golden Girls* from 1985 to 1992. She received the 1988 Emmy Award for Best Actress in a Comedy Series.

RICHARD C. ATKINSON is the president of the University of California. Atkinson served as chancellor of the San Diego campus for fifteen years prior to being appointed to the UC presidency in 1995. He is the coauthor with his wife, Rita, of the textbook *Introduction to Psychology*. During his tenure at University of California at San Diego, Chancellor Atkinson championed the establishment of endowed chairs as an important mechanism for recruiting and retaining top-quality faculty and supporting major research. Since the first chair was established in 1981, the number of endowed chairs had grown to sixty-one by 1997.

BRUCE BABBITT, secretary of the Department of Interior, was appointed by President Clinton. He has developed large-scale, consensus-based environmental restoration projects such as restoring the ecosystems of southern Florida in the Everglades and Florida Bay. In the Pacific Northwest, he helped shape the President's Forest Plan, a multispecies regional plan that protects millions of acres of old-growth forest while providing for a substantial level of timber harvest.

RUSSELL BAKER is a *New York Times* columnist and recipient of the 1982 Pulitzer Prize for his autobiography, *Growing Up*.

ALEC BALDWIN starred in *Mercury Rising* (1998), *Ghosts of Mississippi* (1996), and *Knots Landing* (1979). He is married to Kim Basinger, an Academy Award–winning actress.

RUSSELL BANKS is the author of, among other books, *Searching for Survivors*, *Family Life*, *The Sweet Hereafter*, and *Cloud Splitter*. *The Sweet Hereafter*, about a town coping with the aftermath of a tragic school bus accident that killed many of the community's children, was made into an Oscar-nominated movie in 1997.

SYDNEY BIDDLE BARROWS was convicted of operating a wealthy prostitution ring, which earned her the nickname of "The Mayflower Madam." She merged business and sex to create Cachet—the escort service of choice among affluent, powerful, and prominent men.

DREW BARRYMORE became famous for her role in 1982 as Gertie, the little sister in *E.T.* She also starred in *Boys on the Side* (1995) and *Ever After* (1998).

DOUGLAS J. BENNET has been the president of Wesleyan University since 1995. Before that he was assistant secretary of state for international organization affairs, managing efforts to streamline and improve relations with the United Nations, a post to which he was appointed by President Clinton. Bennet is best known for his decade as chief executive officer and president of National Public Radio; there he succeeded in tripling listenership and nearly doubling the number of member stations, while raising funds to end its nearly total dependence on federal money.

SHELLEY BERMAN is a comedic actor who starred in *The Best Man* (1964) and *The Blob* (1972).

RAY BILLINGSLEY is a cartoonist who created *Curtis*, which appears in more than 250 newspapers. He finds inspiration for the strip in his own childhood memories and in life at the local barbershop, where friends talk about everything from small-town gossip to big fantasies and problems.

BONNIE BLAIR, a speed skater, won six Olympic medals, including five golds. She is America's most winning athlete in Winter Olympic history and is the only U.S. Winter Olympian to win gold medals in the same event in three consecutive Olympics.

NICOLAAS BLOEMBERGEN received the 1981 Nobel Prize in Physics for his "contribution to the development of laser spectroscopy," the physics that deals with the interpretation of the interactions between matter and radiation.

MALCOLM A. BORG is CEO of the *Bergen* (New Jersey) *Record*. He is the recipient of the 1985 Editor of Year Award from the National Press Photographers Association, which recognizes outstanding editorship.

RAY BRADBURY is a novelist, short story writer, playwright, essayist, screenwriter, and poet who has written over fifty books, including *Fahrenheit 451* (1953), *The Autumn People* (1965), and *The Martian Chronicles* (1950). His animated film about the history of flight, *Icarus Montgolfier Wright*, was nominated for an Academy Award, and his teleplay of *The Halloween Tree* earned an Emmy.

DAVID BRENNER, a comedian, hosted his own late night talk show, *Highlife*. He has made numerous appearances on *The Tonight Show* and appears regularly on *The Late Show with David Letterman* and *Late Night with Conan O'Brien*.

JAMES M. BUCHANAN, JR., received the 1986 Nobel Prize in Economics for his development of the contractual and constitutional bases for the theory of economic and political decision making. He has become the leading researcher in the field, which has come to be known as "public choice theory."

PATRICK J. BUCHANAN, the candidate for the Republican presidential nomination in 1992, ran on a platform of judicial reform and strict immigration control. He deems American society overregulated and overtaxed by government.

BARBARA BUSH, universally known as a sensible, down-to-earth person, was an enormously popular First Lady from 1989 to 1993. In addition to her many duties, she crusaded against illiteracy and supported programs to help the homeless and fight child abuse. Among her many affiliations with literacy groups, she continues as an honorary sponsor of Laubauch Literacy Volunteers and is a member of the National Advisory Council of Literacy Volunteers of America, Inc. She was raised in Rye, New York, and graduated from Smith College.

GEORGE BUSH, a Republican, was the forty-first president of the United States from 1989 to 1993 and vice president from 1981 to 1989 under Ronald Reagan. He is a graduate of Yale University and was director of the Central Intelligence Agency in 1976 and 1977.

ROBERT C. BYRD has been a Democratic senator from West Virginia since 1959. He enjoys the distinction of having held more leadership positions in the U.S. Senate than any other senator of any party in history. In 1994, Senator Byrd was elected to a seventh consecutive six-year term, making him one of only three senators in American history to achieve that milestone.

ROBERT CAMPBELL received the 1996 Pulitzer Prize in Criticism for his knowledgeable writing on architecture. He is a practicing architect in Cambridge, Massachusetts. The architecture critic of *The Boston Globe*, he has published more than seventy feature articles in national periodicals and is currently a contributing editor of the magazine *Architectural Record*.

GEORGE CARLIN is a comedian most famous for his list of "Seven Words You Can't Say on Television." When HBO came along, he finally got the opportunity to say them to the world.

RICHARD CARPENTER, with his sister, Karen, formed the duo the Carpenters. They made their debut in November 1969 and with only their second release, "Close to You," reached the top of the American charts. Richard Carpenter has won three Grammy Awards.

BARBARA CARTLAND has been called the world's best-known author of romantic fiction. Her books have sold over 650 million copies worldwide. She is listed in *The Guinness Book of World Records* as the world's top-selling author.

JOHNNY CASH is a country music superstar. He has recorded more than 1500 songs on 500 albums and has placed 48 singles on the *Billboard* Hot 100 pop charts, which is the same number as the Rolling Stones. With more pop hit singles than Michael Jackson or the Supremes, he is one of the very few people in the history of music to sell more than 50 million records. In 1969, when Cash was at his zenith, he was the hottest act in the world, selling more than 250,000 albums a month, outselling even the Beatles. Cash has won nine Grammy Awards, the most recent for Best Country Album in 1998 for *Unchained.*

JOHN H. CHAFEE, Republican senator from Rhode Island, was elected to the U.S. Senate in 1976 and was reelected to a fourth term in 1994. As chairman of the Environment and Public Works Committee, the senator was a leading voice in crafting the Clean Air Act of 1990, which strengthened pollution emission standards.

TOM CLANCY is an internationally bestselling author. Most of his ten complex techothriller books have held the number one position on the *New York Times* bestseller list. He is regularly welcomed aboard jets, destroyers, and submarines to research his fiction. Admirals and generals give him access, Pentagon officials debrief him, and many of his books are required reading at American war colleges. His novels include *Clear and Present Danger* (1994), *Patriot Games* (1992), and *The Hunt for Red October* (1990), among more than a dozen others.

MAX CLELAND, Democratic senator from Georgia, was elected to the U.S. Senate in 1996 and is leading efforts to make improvements in health care for members and retirees of the armed forces and their families. In 1996, he was named to *Time*'s list of rising Democrats.

MICHAEL T. COHEN is president of Williams Real Estate Company, Inc., in New York City.

NATALIE COLE, the daughter of jazz and pop legend Nat "King" Cole, has had a twophase career—the first in rhythm and blues and urban contemporary music, and the second in jazz-based pop. She won Grammy Awards for Best New Artist and Best R&B Female Vocalist in 1975. She has sold nearly 35 million albums worldwide.

KENT CONRAD, Democratic senator from North Dakota, was elected to the U.S. Senate in 1986 and again in 1994. He has focused on maintaining the world's strongest military and providing key retirement, health-care, and other benefits to our nation's military personnel. In 1968, as a teenager, he headed up a statewide campaign to grant voting rights to nineteen-year-olds.

DENTON A. COOLEY performed the first successful human heart transplantation in 1968 at the Texas Heart Institute. Dr. Cooley is president and surgeon-in-chief of the Texas Heart Institute at St. Luke's Episcopal Hospital, which he founded in 1962. Dr. Cooley and his associates have performed more then ninety-three thousand open-heart operations—more then any other group in the world. Throughout his career, Cooley has received numerous honors and awards, including the Medal of Freedom, the nation's highest civilian award, presented by President Reagan in 1984.

KATIE COURIC has been coanchor of NBC's *The Today Show* since 1991. She began her television broadcasting career with CNN as an assistant on the assignment desk in Washington, D.C. When she was a general assignment reporter with WRC-TV, the NBC station in Washington, she won an Emmy and an Associated Press award for her story about a dating service for handicapped people.

JENNY CRAIG founded Jenny Craig, Inc., one of the largest weight management service companies in the world. A fitness guru, Craig has published numerous books on health, and Jenny Craig, Inc., produces home exercise videos and other weight management products.

BRIAN CRANE is a cartoonist who created the nationally syndicated *Pickles*, a comic strip that deals with the ups and downs of getting older.

MARIO CUOMO was the Democratic governor of New York from 1983 to 1995. During his term, he created more than half a million jobs for New Yorkers and led the state through two national recessions. He gained notoriety with his eloquent keynote address at the 1984 Democratic Convention and is mentioned as a possible candidate for the U.S. Supreme Court.

CLIVE CUSSLER is the author of fifteen novels, including *Flood Tide* (1998), *Raise the Titanic* (1980), and *Iceberg* (1975). He is also the discoverer of over sixty historic shipwrecks, including the long-lost Confederate submarine *Hunley* and LaSalle's ship *L'Aimable*.

CHUCK DALY is one of the most renowned basketball coaches in the NBA. He coached the Cleveland Cavaliers (1981–82), Detroit Pistons (1983–92), and New Jersey Nets (1992–94). He was also coach of the 1992 U.S. Olympic Dream Team. He was elected to the Basketball Hall of Fame in 1994 and is currently a network broadcaster at TNT.

ALFONSE M. D'AMATO was a Republican senator from New York and served from 1980 to 1998. Since 1992, he has fought for and won over $750 million in federal funding for breast cancer research. He has also led the fight to restore to Holocaust survivors and the heirs of victims the assets that were deposited in Swiss banks prior to World War II.

MICHAEL E. DEBAKEY is a cardiovascular surgeon known for inventing and perfecting numerous medical devices, techniques, and procedures, including Dacron arteries, arterial bypass operations, artificial hearts, heart pumps, and heart transplants. He has served as a health-care adviser to almost every U.S. president in the last fifty years. He is also credited with developing the Mobile Army Surgical Hospital (M.A.S.H.) concept for the military, which saved thousands of lives during the Korean and Vietnam wars.

LOIS B. DEFLEUR was the president of Columbia University from 1986 to 1990 and has been the president of the State University of New York at Binghamton since 1990.

OSCAR DE LA RENTA is a high-fashion designer who is best known for his classic clothing and fragrances for men and women.

DOM DELUISE is a director and actor. He starred in *Cannonball Run II* (1984) and *Smokey and the Bandit II* (1980). He has also done voice work for many recent Disney animated movies.

NELSON DEMILLE is the author of more than a dozen hit books including *Plum Island* (1997), *The Charm School* (1988), and *The Cathedral* (1981). While serving in the military, he earned an Air Medal and a Bronze Star.

JOHN A. DIBIAGGIO has been president of Tufts University since 1992.

JEANE DIXON, known as "Astrologer to the Stars," has had many famous clients. Dixon became famous for predicting an infamous event: In a 1956 interview, she stated that a Democratic president, elected in 1960, would die in office. After President Kennedy's assassination, she became known as the "Seeress of Washington." According to Dixon, who went on to write a syndicated column, she told interviewers that the president would be assassinated, but they refused to publish her words.

ROBERT J. DOLE was a Republican senator from Kansas and was the vice-presidential candidate in 1976 and the presidential candidate in 1996.

MICHAEL S. DUKAKIS was the 1988 Democratic candidate for president and lost the election to George Bush. As a Massachusetts state legislator in 1970, Dukakis introduced a bill to legalize abortion in Massachusetts three years prior to the *Roe* v. *Wade* Supreme Court decision, which legalized abortion nationwide. As a presidential candidate, Dukakis ran on a platform that called abortion "the fundamental right of reproductive choice" and supported federal funding of abortion.

DOMINICK DUNNE is the author of potboiler novels that are based on real-life high-society scandals, including *The Two Mrs. Grenvilles, An Inconvenient Woman,* and *A Season in Purgatory.* He is a contributing editor to *Vanity Fair.*

RICHARD J. DURBIN is a Democratic senator from Illinois who was elected in 1996. During his previous twelve-year service in the House of Representatives, he took on the tobacco industry and won passage of landmark legislation to ban smoking on commercial airline flights.

MICHAEL EISNER has been the chairman and chief executive officer of the Walt Disney Company since 1984, when he averted the dissolution of Disney by takeover sharks. In 1964, as an NBC clerk, Eisner earned $65 a week in the page program. Though he took only one business course in his life—accounting—he managed to rise to heights that earned him over half a billion dollars in 1997 and earned over $80 billion for Disney stockholders. He is the author of the autobiography *Work in Progress.*

GERTRUDE B. ELION is the 1988 Nobel Prize recipient in Medicine for the discovery of important principles for drug treatment. Over the years, her research philosophy has formed the basis for the development of new drugs against a variety of diseases.

JAN ELIOT created the syndicated cartoon strip *Stone Soup,* which reflects the world of the nineties: single mothers, working moms, independent women of all ages, not-so-independent women, "new" men, and not-so-new men.

CHRIS EVERT is a tennis champion who won eighteen Grand Slam singles titles: two titles at the Australian Open, seven titles at the French Open, three titles at

Wimbledon, and six titles at the U.S. Open. Her ranking was never lower than number four in all seventeen years she played tennis professionally. She was unanimously inducted into the International Tennis Hall of Fame on July 16, 1995.

JERRY L. FALWELL is one of the most powerful leaders of the religious right. He loudly proclaims himself a fundamentalist and a spokesman for the Christian faith. In 1983, Falwell was named one of *Time*'s "Top 25 Most Influential People in America." The founder of Liberty University (in 1971), he received an award as Christian Humanitarian of the Year in 1983.

GERALDINE A. FERRARO was the first woman vice-presidential nominee on the Democratic ticket. She has been a teacher and a mother, a prosecutor and a Member of Congress and an ambassador, as well as a vigorous advocate for progressive values. Ferraro has remained an active participant in foreign affairs and was appointed by President Clinton to be the U.S. ambassador to the United Nations Human Rights Commission.

COTTON FITZSIMMONS is a professional basketball executive who received the NBA Coach of the Year Award in 1979 and 1989. He has been the senior executive vice president of the Phoenix Suns since 1992.

GERALD R. FORD was vice president of the United States under Richard Nixon and thirty-ninth president of the United States from 1974 to 1977. In the aftermath of the Watergate scandal, he was the first vice president chosen under the terms of the Twenty-fifth Amendment, which says that in case of the removal or resignation of the president from office, the vice president shall become president. A native of Grand Rapids, Michigan, Ford starred on the University of Michigan football team, then went to Yale, where he served as assistant coach while earning his law degree. During World War II, he attained the rank of lieutenant commander in the navy. After the war, he returned to Grand Rapids, where he practiced law and entered Republican politics.

WENDELL H. FORD has been a Democratic senator from Kentucky since 1974. He introduced the first-ever program for the use of recycled printing paper by the federal government and was successful in cutting millions of dollars from government printing operations.

JAMES O. FREEDMAN was president of Dartmouth College from 1987 to 1998. A legal scholar, he clerked for Thurgood Marshall and was an associate with the New York law firm of Paul, Weiss, Rifkind, Wharton, and Garrison. At Dartmouth, he oversaw the development of numerous academic initiatives, including reinstating Japanese and Hebrew and instituting studies in Arabic, Latin America, and the Caribbean. Freedman is the author of *Idealism and Liberal Education* and was elected in 1998 to the American Academy of Arts and Sciences for his contributions to scholastic and public affairs.

ANDY GARCIA starred in *Desperate Measures* (1998), *Hero* (1992), and *The Godfather: Part III* (1990). He received Academy Award and Golden Globe nominations for his role as Vincent Mancini in *The Godfather: Part III* and was voted Star of the Year by the National Association of Theater Owners for his performances in it and in *Internal Affairs*. Born in Havana, Cuba, Garcia was exiled with his family to Miami Beach, Florida, at the age of five. He attended Florida International University and spent several years performing in regional theater productions before moving to Los Angeles in the late 1970s.

ART GARFUNKEL is a singer and songwriter who, with his partner, Paul Simon, won seven Grammy Awards, including Record of the Year in 1969 for *Mrs. Robinson*.

ESTELLE GETTY starred in the long-running television sitcom *The Golden Girls* and the hit movie *Tootsie* (1983).

TERRY GILLIAM directed *Twelve Monkeys* (1995) and *The Fisher King* (1991), which was nominated for four Academy Awards and won several awards from the Los Angeles Film Critics Association.

RUTH BADER GINSBURG is a Supreme Court justice appointed by President Clinton. Her appointment was confirmed by the Senate 97–3, and she was sworn in as the second female Supreme Court justice of the United States on August 10, 1993. She has earned the reputation of being a "balanced jurist."

RUDOLPH W. GIULIANI, the Republican mayor of New York City since 1994, is credited with reducing crime and restoring a high quality of life to the city.

DANNY GLOVER starred in *Lethal Weapon 4* (1998), *The Color Purple* (1985), and *Escape From Alcatraz* (1979), among many other movies. Born and raised in San Francisco, Glover trained at the Black Actor Workshop of the American Conservatory Theatre. He has been appointed the first United Nations development programme goodwill ambassador.

JANE GOODALL is an anthropologist known for her groundbreaking studies on chimpanzees. She is the author of *My Friends, the Wild Chimpanzees* (1967). After more than thirty-five consecutive years of research, much of it in the field in

Africa, she continues to contribute significant findings on chimpanzee behavior. She founded the Jane Goodall Institute, which is intended for wildlife research, education, and conservation.

BARRY GOSIN is the CEO of Newmark & Company Real Estate, Inc., a full-service commercial leasing and management company in New York City. It has almost a hundred brokers and a management portfolio in excess of thirty-one million square feet.

NEIL R. GRABOIS has been president of Colgate University since 1988.

VARTAN GREGORIAN was president of Brown University from 1989 to 1996. He then went on to become president of the Carnegie Corporation. Before taking his post at Brown, Gregorian was president and CEO of the New York Public Library, where he raised $400 million and helped to restore the stature of public libraries around the country.

CHARLES GRODIN starred in *Dave* (1993), *Midnight Run* (1988), and *The Heartbreak Kid* (1972).

BUDDY HACKETT is an actor and comedian who starred in *Scrooged* (1988), *The Music Man* (1962), and *Fireman Save My Child* (1954).

MONTY HALL is a television producer and actor who was the host of *Let's Make a Deal* (1964), and *Keep Talking* (1958).

MARVIN HAMLISCH, a composer, was the first person to win three Academy Awards in one evening when he took home Oscars for Best Original Score and Best Original Song for *The Way We Were* and Best Adapted Score for his arrangement of Scott Joplin's music for *The Sting*.

JOHN C. HARSANYI is the 1994 Nobel Prize recipient in Economics for his pioneering analysis of equilibria in the theory of noncooperative games.

GARY HART was the Democratic senator from Colorado from 1976 to 1984. He ran for the Democratic presidential nomination in 1988 and lost to Michael Dukakis after his extramarital affair to Donna Rice was disclosed to the public.

PAUL HARVEY has been a syndicated columnist for the Los AngelesTimes Syndicate since 1954. The ABC Radio Network broadcasts him to twenty-three million listeners via more than twelve hundred radio stations across the U.S.A.

ORRIN G. HATCH is a Republican senator from Utah. As the chairman of the Senate Judiciary Committee, he is an advocate of tougher anticrime laws, civil justice reform to unclog the courts, and legislation to protect individual property rights.

THOMAS K. HEARN, JR., has been president of Wake Forest University since 1983. Wake Forest is a private four-year institution located in North Carolina that is committed to the ideals of a liberal arts education.

HOWELL HEFLIN was a Democratic senator from Alabama from 1979 to 1996. He expanded funding for technology and medical research and wrote the law that protects researchers from terrorist threats and other menacing acts.

JESSE HELMS, a Republican senator from North Carolina since 1973, has repeatedly tied Congress in knots over his amendments to kill the National Endowment for the Arts (NEA). As a result, Helms has been branded by his critics as "Senator No."

LEONA M. HELMSLEY is president and chief executive of Helmsley-Spear, Inc., a five-billion-dollar real estate empire that owns hotels and commercial properties and is based in New York. In March 1992, Helmsley was sentenced to four years' imprisonment for tax evasion.

BUNNY HOEST is the creator of the cartoon *The Lockhorns*.

ROALD HOFFMANN received the 1981 Nobel Prize in Chemistry for his study of the electronic structure of molecules and how they might react and whether they are stable conductors. He teaches at Cornell University.

ERNEST F. HOLLINGS, Democratic senator from South Carolina since 1966, waged a well-known fight to cut the federal deficit, lower the national debt, and eliminate wasteful spending.

LARRY HOLMES is a former World Boxing Confederation Heavyweight Champion (1978–1985) and a former International Boxing Federation Heavyweight Champion. One of twelve children, Holmes quit school at thirteen to work at a car wash and to shine shoes to make money for his family. In his first pro fight in 1973, Holmes was paid $63. Now, Holmes is Easton, Pennsylvania's most successful entrepreneur with $13 million in real estate holdings, including a nightclub and a restaurant. After retiring twice, Holmes surprised the world by coming back to fight in 1994, ranking as one of the top ten heavyweights in the world. At forty-seven, he had an incredible 66–6 record, including forty-two knockouts.

LOU HOLTZ, head coach of the Notre Dame Fighting Irish since 1986, received the National Coach of the Year award in 1988.

DAVID HOROWITZ is a consumer advocate who has won fifteen Emmy Awards in consumer reporting.

KIM HUNTER starred in *The Kindred* (1987), *Escape from the Planet of the Apes* (1971), and *Anything Can Happen* (1952).

HENRY JAGLOM directed *Last Summer in the Hamptons* (1995) and *Sitting Ducks* (1980).

LYNN JOHNSTON created the nationally syndicated cartoon *For Better or for Worse.* Her comic strip deals with the life and times of the Patterson family.

BARBARA JORDAN, in 1966, became the first black woman to win a seat in the Texas Senate. During her tenure, she defended the cause of the poor and promoted civil rights legislation. Later, as a member of the House Judiciary Committee, she earned national attention for her eloquent speech in favor of impeaching President Richard M. Nixon during the Watergate hearings.

NAOMI JUDD is the recipient of seven Grammy Awards for hits such as "Why Not Me," "Turn It Loose," and "Girls Night Out."

MICHAEL KARIN is a professor of pharmacology at the School of Medicine of the University of California at San Diego. He is most famous for his research in gene expression.

JACK KEMP was Bob Dole's running mate in the 1996 election. He was named chairman of the National Committee on Economic Growth and Tax Reform by Dole and House Speaker Newt Gingrich to study how a restructuring of the tax code could help expand the economy without inflation. Kemp is president of the board of Empower America, a public advocacy organization he cofounded in 1993 with William Bennett, Jeanne Kirkpatrick, and Vim Weber. It is dedicated to "expanding freedom and democractic capitalism around the world, promoting policies to expand economic growth, job creation . . . and advancing social policies which empower people, not bureaucratic governments."

EDWARD M. KENNEDY has been a Democratic senator from Massachusetts since 1962. With President Clinton, he has pledged to push for legislation that would expand access to health coverage for uninsured children and has supported legislation concerning immigration, labor, and human rights.

J. ROBERT KERREY, a Democratic senator from Nebraska since 1989, is a former Navy SEAL. During the Vietnam War he earned the Congressional Medal of Honor, America's highest military honor.

NANCY KERRIGAN is an Olympic figure skater. She earned the silver medal at Lillehammer in 1994, the bronze medal at the 1991 Figure Skating Championships, and was the U.S. National Champion in 1993.

BILLIE JEAN KING is a tennis champion who won over ten career grand slam titles and was the first woman commentator in the history of professional tennis. She is also cofounder of *WomenSports* magazine and was named *Time* magazine's Woman of the Year in 1976.

KENNETH W. KINZLER is a professor of oncology and pharmacology and molecular sciences at Johns Hopkins University. Kinzler was instrumental in the discovery of the gene mutation that is believed to cause inherited colorectol cancer, which accounts for between 15 and 25 percent of all cases of colon cancer. A graduate of the doctoral program at Johns Hopkins University, Kinzler is devoted to understanding the genetic changes that underlie the development of human cancer.

EDWARD I. KOCH was New York City's feisty, populist mayor from 1978 to 1989. A public speaker, he is also the author of nine books, including three mysteries, and the host of *The People's Court.*

DEAN KOONTZ is a bestselling author of more than fifty-nine novels, including *Watchers Reborn* (1998), *Hideaway* (1992), and *Demon Seed* (1973).

BRIAN J. LALINE is editor of the *Staten Island Advance.*

FRANK LAUTENBERG is the Democratic senator from New Jersey who introduced laws to ban the ocean dumping of sludge and plastics and helped write the Clean Air and Safe Drinking Water acts.

NORMAN LEAR produced and directed *Fried Green Tomatoes* (1991), *The Baxters* (1979), and the hit television show *All in the Family,* which ran from 1971 until 1979.

DAVID M. LEE received, with Douglas Osheroff, the 1996 Nobel Prize in Physics for the discovery of superfluidity in helium-3, a breakthrough in low-temperature physics.

WASSILY LEONTIEF received the 1973 Nobel Prize in Economics for his creation of the input-output theory. He defined input as the goods and services that each industry buys from all the other industries and output as the products each industry sells to the others. Economists use his method to analyze, plan, and predict economic changes.

RICHARD C. LEVIN, president of Yale University since 1993, is also an economics professor interested in industrial research and development and intellectual property.

SHARI LEWIS, puppeteer, ventriloquist, and children's entertainer, was the recipient of eleven Emmy Awards.

G. GORDON LIDDY was the driving force behind the Watergate break-in that erupted into the greatest scandal in the history of American politics. Liddy claimed that he broke into the Democratic National Committee headquarters in June 1972 not to place bugging devices on telephones of DNC officials but to obtain information on a call-girl ring being operated out of the DNC's Watergate office.

ART LINKLETTER is a television and radio personality who starred for more than sixty years in two of the longest running shows in broadcast history, *The Art Linkletter Show* (1963) and *People Are Funny* (1954).

SHELLEY LONG, an actress, is most famous for her role as Diane Chambers on *Cheers*, for which she earned a 1983 Emmy as Best Lead Actress in a Comedy Series. She has been nominated for four Emmys and is the recipient of two Golden Globe Awards, all for her lead comedic role in *Cheers* (1982–1987). She also starred in the movie *The Money Pit* (1986).

TRENT LOTT, a Republican senator from Mississippi since 1989, is known for his opposition to gun control bills. He is a cosponsor of legislation that will increase the penalties for violent crimes, streamline the appeals process, and fund prison construction.

RICHARD G. LUGAR, Republican senator from Indiana since 1977, has stated that his vision for America is to reinvigorate our traditional values of religious faith, family, honesty, and integrity and to secure the country from the threat of attack by weapons of mass destruction.

JOHN McCAIN has been a Republican senator from Arizona since 1987. In 1997, Senator McCain was named one of *Time* magazine's "Top 25 Most Influential People in America." As a P.O.W. in Vietnam for five and a half years, he was awarded the Silver Star, Bronze Star, Legion of Merit, Purple Heart, and the Distinguished Flying Cross.

FRANK McCORMICK is the director of the University of California at San Francisco's Cancer Center & Cancer Research Institute, a leader in cancer research. McCormick is interested in how viruses and cells interact, using gene display methods to identify host genes that are turned on or off by viral infections. He intends to use this information to design new generations of viruses with cancer specificity.

KILMER McCULLY, a pioneering pathologist, claims that our vitamin B–depleted food supply may be the culprit behind the epidemic of heart disease. He discovered that vitamin B deficiency can cause the buildup of homocysteine, an amino acid, and lead to strokes and heart attacks. McCully's research points to how diet and lifestyle can compensate for these deficiencies.

JOHN W. MARTIN, JR., is a lawyer who has been vice president and general counsel and senior attorney of the Ford Motor Company since 1989.

ROBERT C. MERTON received the 1997 Nobel Prize in Economics for a new method to determine the value of derivatives.

SHANNON MILLER was a member of the first Gold Medal Olympic Gymnastics Team in 1996. Her total Olympic medal count now stands at two gold, two silver, and three bronze. She has won more Olympic and World Championship medals than any other American gymnast, male or female, in history. She is the only American in history to win two consecutive World Championship all-around titles. Miller began gymnastics in 1982. Her favorite apparatuses are the uneven bars and balance beam. She spent seven years on the U.S. National Team and is currently a student at the University of Oklahoma.

DANIEL PATRICK MOYNIHAN was a Democratic senator from New York, elected in 1977, who led the first comprehensive review in forty years of the federal government's system of classifying and declassifying information and granting security clearances.

KATHY NAJIMY starred in *Veronica's Closet* (1997) and *Sister Act* (1992).

SAM NEILL starred in *The Horse Whisperer* (1998), *Jurassic Park* (1993), and *The Hunt for Red October* (1990).

BOB NEWHART starred in *The Bob Newhart Show* (1972), *Catch-22* (1970), and *Hell Is for Heroes* (1962). He was named to the Academy Hall of Fame in 1993. His eponymous hit show depicted the life of Bob Hartley, a Chicago psychologist, and his wife, Emily, played by Suzanne Pleshette.

LESLIE NIELSEN, a comedic actor, starred in *Wrongfully Accused* (1998), *Spy Hard* (1996), *Naked Gun 33 1/3: The Final Insult* (1994), and *Airplane!* (1980).

OLIVER NORTH is a nationally syndicated radio broadcaster and newspaper columnist. A combat-decorated Marine, he was indicted for defrauding the U.S. government for his role in the Iran/Contra Affair in 1988. According to José Blandon, an aide to Panama's strongman, Manuel Noriega, North had two meetings with Noriega in 1985. Even though Washington knew Noriega was involved in the international drug trade, Blandon alleges North pledged to help obtain U.S. aid to ease Panama's foreign debt crisis. In return, Noriega promised to help in setting up two Contra training camps in Panama.

JOHN CARDINAL O'CONNOR has been archbishop of New York since 1984.

SANDRA DAY O'CONNOR, a Supreme Court justice, was appointed by President Reagan in 1981, becoming the first woman ever to sit on the Supreme Court. She has been noted as being generally conservative, but she frequently surprises observers with her political independence.

GEORGE A. OLAH received the 1994 Nobel Prize in Chemistry for revolutionizing the study of hydrocarbons and uncovering new ways to use them in the petroleum industry. He teaches at the University of Southern California.

DOUGLAS D. OSHEROFF shared the 1996 Nobel Prize in Physics with David Lee for the discovery of superfluidity in helium-3, a breakthrough in low-temperature physics.

REGIS PHILBIN co-hosts the daytime talk show *Live with Regis and Kathie Lee*. He has been in front of the camera for thirty-five years, and has made guest appearances on *Seinfeld, Mad About You, Diagnosis Murder*, and *Perry Mason: The Case of the Tell-Tale Talk Show Host*. A graduate of Notre Dame University, Philbin has served as an anchor, news reporter, news and sports writer. He is the author of *I'm Only One Man* and has been nominated seven times for an Emmy Award.

ROBERT PINSKY was named the thirty-ninth United States poet laureate in 1997. A prize-winning poet, essayist, and translator, Pinsky propelled Dante onto best-seller lists with his acclaimed 1994 verse translation of *The Inferno*. Pinsky teaches in the Graduate Writing Program at Boston University and is a regular contributor to *The NewsHour with Jim Lehrer*. Poetry editor of the weekly Internet magazine *Slate*, his awards and nominations include the Los Angeles Times Book Award, the William Carlos Williams Prize, and the Pulitzer Prize. He began his artistic career as a saxophone player, but switched to poetry in college.

ROMAN POLANSKI wrote and directed *Frantic* (1988), *Tess* (1980), *Chinatown* (1974), and *Rosemary's Baby* (1968). Polanski has acted in *Grosse Fatigue* (1994), *Back in the U.S.S.R.* (1992), and *The Fearless Vampire Killers* (1967). His awards include the Venice Film Festival Critics' Prize Award, the Golden Globe Award, and the Los Angeles Film Critics Award for Best Director.

PAULA POUNDSTONE, a comedian, starred in *The Paula Poundstone Show* (1993). She writes the "Poundstone Report" for *Mother Jones* magazine, is the producer and voice on the children's audio book *Completely Yours*, and serves as the roving reporter for *The Rosie O'Donnell Show*. Her awards include the Cable Ace Award, Academy Comedy Award, and an Emmy. An advocate and champion of children's rights, she became a foster parent in 1993.

DAN QUAYLE, a former Indiana senator, served as vice president of the United States from 1989 to 1993 in the Bush administration. Quayle began his career in politics as a member of the House of Representatives at age twenty-nine. His chairmanships include the National Space Council and President's Council on Competitiveness. He pioneered the national conversation on family values with his infamous "Murphy Brown" speech in 1992. He is the author of *Standing Firm*.

HUNTER R. RAWLINGS III has served as the president of Cornell University since 1995. A Virginia native and classics scholar, Rawlings received his Ph.D. in 1970 from Princeton University and is the author of *A Semantic Study of Prophasis to 400 B.C.* and *The Structure of Thucydides' History*.

WILLIS REED is the executive vice president of the New Jersey Nets. As a player for both the New Jersey Nets and New York Knicks, Reed was named NBA Rookie of the Year 1964–1965 (the first Knicks player ever to accomplish this) and has appeared in seven All Star Games. Reed was elected to the NBA Hall of Fame in 1971, was NBA Most Valuable Player 1969–1970, and was named one of "50 Greatest Players in NBA History" in 1997.

JANET RENO is the first female attorney general of the United States. A graduate of Cornell University and Harvard University Law School, Reno has been instrumental in reducing the nation's crime and violence rates and enforcing civil rights. She is an avid canoer and hiker.

EDWARD A. RIGUARDI is chairman of Colliers ABR., Inc., a commercial real-estate services firm headquartered in New York City. Through its international partnership, its reach extends to 215 offices in forty-four countries. It manages three hundred million square feet of real estate and completes transactions valued at $16 billion annually.

GERALDO RIVERA, a journalist, has hosted *Geraldo, Geraldo Live,* and *20/20.* The recipient of seven Emmy Awards, Rivera has appeared in the film *Contact* and on television in *Perry Mason: The Case of the Ruthless Romeo.*

PAT ROBERTS, a Republican senator from Kansas, wrote the Freedom to Farm law, which gained national acclaim for being the most pro-environment farm bill ever enacted. Roberts has served eight terms in the House of Representatives and on four Senate committees: Agriculture, Nutrition and Forestry; Armed Services; Intelligence; and Ethics. In the Senate, he champions government that is less involved in Kansans' lives and pocketbooks.

JUDITH RODIN has been president of the University of Pennsylvania since 1994. A noted researcher and psychologist, Rodin is professor of psychology at Penn's School of Arts and Sciences and professor of medicine and psychiatry at the university's School of Medicine. She had been provost of Yale University since 1992. She is the author of *Body Traps: Breaking the Binds That Keep You from Feeling Good About Your Body,* among other books. A native Philadelphian, Rodin graduated from the University of Pennsylvania and received her doctorate from Columbia University.

FRED ROGERS has been the producer and star of PBS's children's television show *Mister Rogers' Neighborhood* since 1965. Rogers began his career as an assistant producer for NBC. He developed and produced *The Children's Corner* in Pittsburgh and then went on to study child development and attend the Pittsburgh Theological Seminary during his off-duty hours. He was ordained by Pittsburgh Presbytery in 1962 with a charge to continue his work with children and families through the media. Now in its third decade, *Mister Rogers' Neighborhood* helps "children find within themselves the courage to grow." Rogers has received honorary degrees from over thirty colleges and universities including Yale University, Carnegie-Mellon University, and Boston University.

GEORGE RUPP has been president of Columbia University since 1993. At Columbia, Rupp is committed to strengthening the relationship among the campus, the surrounding communities, and New York City. He came to Columbia from the presidency of Rice University, where applications almost tripled and federal research support more than doubled under his charge. Before Rice, Rupp was professor of divinity and dean of the Harvard Divinity School. He is the author of four books including *Beyond Existentialism and Zen: Religion in a Pluralistic World* and *Commitment and Community.*

RENE RUSSO starred in *Lethal Weapon IV* (1998), *Outbreak* (1995), *In the Line of Fire* (1993), *Get Shorty* (1995), and *Ransom* (1996). Russo was discovered by an International Creative Management agent when she was picked out of a crowd at a Los Angeles Forum parking lot. She then became a model with the Ford Modeling Agency.

PAUL A. SAMUELSON received the 1970 Nobel Prize in Economics. A teacher at Stanford University, Samuelson was the first American to win the Nobel Prize in Economics. He is best known for his book *Foundations of Economic Analysis*, which greatly increased the use of mathematics in economics. He has served as president of the American Economic Association and taught at the Massachusetts Institute of Technology.

ARTHUR L. SCHAWLOW received the 1981 Nobel Prize in Physics for his contribution to the development of laser spectroscopy. He was the coinventor with Charles Townes of the optical laser in 1958. He was inducted into the Inventor's Hall of Fame in 1996.

MYRON SCHOLES won the Nobel Memorial Prize in Economic Science in 1997 for "a new method to determine the value of derivatives." His pricing model has become a benchmark formula for the valuation of stock options and has put a fledgling options market on its feet. Scholes has also served as professor of law at Stanford Law School and a senior research fellow at the Hoover Institution. He retired from Stanford in 1997 and now serves as principal and limited partner of Long-Term Capital Management, L.P., a Greenwich, Connecticut, investment management firm. He is professor of finance emeritus at the Stanford Graduate School of Business.

ROBERT L. SHAPIRO is a high-profile defense attorney who has represented celebrity clients such as O. J. Simpson and Darryl Strawberry.

WILLIAM F. SHARPE received the 1990 Nobel Prize in Economics. The Timken professor of finance at Stanford University Graduate School of Business, Sharpe developed the Sharpe Ratio for investment performance analysis, which is a method for valuing options. A past president of the American Finance Association, Sharpe received his Ph.D., M.A., and B.A. in economics from the University of California at Los Angeles.

LIZ SMITH, a gossip columnist for the *New York Daily News*, is a leading literacy advocate.

ROBERT M. SOLOW received the 1987 Nobel Prize in Economics for his analysis of economic growth. A professor at the Massachusetts Institute of Technology, he received his doctorate from Harvard University and wrote *Capital Theory and the Rate of Return* and *Linear Programming and Economic Analysis.* His most provocative theory is that economic growth cannot be explained by increases in capital or labor.

HUGO F. SONNENSCHEIN is the president of the University of Chicago. A prominent economic theorist, his various contributions to economics are dominated by one shattering idea: the Debreu-Sonnenschein-Mantel Theorem, which claims that market demand functions, on which all the "intuitive" results of market-level and macro-level economics rest, are essentially shapeless.

GERRY L. SPENCE, a Wyoming-based criminal defense lawyer, is known for the defense of former Philippines First Lady Imelda Marcos and white separatist Randy Weaver. Spence first gained national recognition when he won a $10.5 million verdict against Kerr-McGee in the Karen Silkwood case. He is the author of *Gunning for Justice, Of Murder and Madness, Trial by Fire, With Justice for None, From Freedom to Slavery,* and his autobiography, *The Making of a Country Lawyer.* Spence has not lost a jury trial since 1969 and has never lost a criminal case.

JACK L. STARK has been president of Claremont McKenna College since 1970. His notable accomplishments include smoothing the college's transition to coeducation in 1976, expanding its academic programs, increasing enrollment by 20 percent, and creating seven new research institutions. He has campaigned to restore a sense of idealism and character among the college's undergraduates and will retire in July 1999.

SY STERNBERG is chairman, president, and CEO of New York Life Insurance Company, one of the largest insurance and financial services companies in the world. Before joining New York Life in 1989, Sternberg served as senior executive vice president and member of the board of directors of the Massachusetts

Mutual Life Insurance Company. A Brooklyn native, he graduated from the City College of New York in 1965 and Northeastern University in 1968.

JON C. STRAUSS has been president of Harvey Mudd College since 1997 and prior to that was vice president and chief financial officer at Howard Hughes Medical Institute. Strauss received his Ph.D. in electrical engineering from Carnegie Institute of Technology, an M.S. in physics from the University of Pittsburgh, and a B.S. in electrical engineering from the University of Wisconsin.

ARTHUR O. SULZBERGER, JR., chairman and publisher of *The New York Times*, comes from an esteemed lineage of publishing mavericks: His grandfather, Arthur Hays Sulzberger, was publisher of the *Times* in 1935, and his father, Arthur Ochs Sulzberger, served as president from 1963 to 1979 and as publisher from 1963 to 1992. Arthur Sulzberger, Jr., became chairman and publisher in 1992 and helped usher in changes such as color printing throughout the daily newspaper.

MOTHER TERESA received the Nobel Peace Prize in 1979. While riding a train to Darjeeling, she received a calling from Jesus to "serve him among the poorest of the poor." In 1937, she took her vows as a nun and spent a lifetime aiding the poor through her Missionaries of Charity and other noble works

STROM THURMOND, a Republican senator from South Carolina, was first elected to the Senate in 1954 as a write-in; he was the first person ever elected to major office in the United States by this method. He serves as president pro tem of the Senate—third in line to succeed the president, following the vice president and the Speaker of the House.

JOHN TRAVOLTA rose to stardom in the 1970s with *Saturday Night Fever* (1977) and *Grease* (1978), and then, after years of obscurity, made a celebrated comeback in Quentin Tarantino's independent hit, *Pulp Fiction* (1994), for which Travolta was nominated for the Best Actor Academy Award.

DONALD TRUMP is a world-famous businessman known for his showiness and real estate holdings. The second son of a contractor, he was raised in New York City and studied finance at the University of Pennsylvania's Wharton School of Business. Trump's billion-dollar empire includes Trump Tower, Trump Plaza, the Empire State Building, the New Jersey Generals, Trump Hotels and Casino Resorts, and the Miss Universe pageant. He is the author of *Trump: The Art of the Comeback, Trump: The Art of Survival, Trump: The Art of the Deal,* and *Trump: Surviving at the Top.*

TED TURNER is an entertainment mogul. He was born in Cincinnati, Ohio, where his family owned a billboard business, but instead of following in his father's footsteps, Turner acquired television station Channel 17, which showed no original programming and minimal news. Within three years, he turned it into a profitable venture with a nationwide audience by airing reruns of classic shows and black-and-white movies. Turner's empire has grown to encompass TBS, the Atlanta Braves, CNN, and the Goodwill Games. He also serves as vice chairman of Time Warner, Inc., which acquired Turner's empire in 1997. He is married to actress and environmentalist Jane Fonda.

DESMOND M. TUTU received the Nobel Peace Prize in 1984 for his work fighting against apartheid. He is the bishop of Johannesburg and former secretary general of the South African Council of Churches, as well as a  professor and ordained deacon. The author of *The African Prayer Book* and *Christianity Amidst Apartheid*, he has received numerous honorary doctorates from Harvard University, Columbia University, King's College in London, and Howard University.

FREDERIQUE VAN DER WAL, a Victoria's Secret model, has appeared on numerous catalogue covers and posed for various posters. A native of Holland, she started her modeling career in the prestigious Elite "Look of the Year" contest. She landed a contract with Elite,  but opted to complete her college education, after which she moved to New York and began her modeling career in earnest. She has since used her business savvy to launch her own line of lingerie, a workout video, a collection of bath products, and Frederique fragrance.

JEFF VAN GUNDY has been head coach of the New York Knickerbockers basketball team since 1997.

DIANA CHAPMAN WALSH was named the president of Wellesley College in 1993. She holds a Ph.D. in public health policy. As a Kellogg National Fellow, she studied workplace democracy and leadership principles around the world.

JOHN WARNER is a Republican senator from Virginia. First elected to the Senate in 1978, he was reelected to serve his fourth six-year term in 1996. In 1991, at the request of President George Bush and Senator Bob Dole, Warner was a leader in the effort to secure the Senate's approval to dispatch the U.S. military during Operation Desert Storm.  Senator Warner is known for being in the forefront of congressional efforts to provide the United States with effective missile defense systems.

ANNIE WELLS received the 1997 Pulitzer Prize for Spot News Photo for her photograph of a firefighter rescuing a teenage girl from swirling flood waters when Wells worked for the *Santa Rosa Press Democrat*. A staff photographer for the *Los Angeles Times* Valley Edition, Wells calls herself "a people photographer," and her images reflect her deep passion and feeling for people's lives and the circumstances surrounding them.

PAUL DAVID WELLSTONE is a Democratic senator from Minnesota. He led the successful fight to raise the federal minimum wage, and he supported legislation that would protect the security of thousands of Minnesotans and their families by preventing corporations from raiding seniors' pension funds.

VANNA WHITE has been the letter-turning cohost on *Wheel of Fortune* since 1975.

SIMON WIESENTHAL is a humanitarian. Born in Buczaz, which is now part of Ukraine, he survived the Nazi death camps and trained as an architect, but he has devoted his life to being a Nazi hunter. In 1977 he founded the Simon Wiesenthal Center, which has offices throughout the world, to carry on the "continuing fight against bigotry and antisemitism."

MONTEL WILLIAMS is host of *The Montel Williams Show*.

TOM WILSON is a cartoonist who created the nationally syndicated *Ziggy* in 1971.

OPRAH WINFREY is an award-winning actress and the host of *The Oprah Winfrey Show*. She starred in *Beloved* (1998), *Native Son* (1986), and *The Color Purple* (1985).

DAVID L. WOLPER produced the first television program ever to be nominated for an Academy Award, *The Race for Space* (1958), which chronicled the American and Russian space programs. Documentary specials that explore the human condition became his trademark, including such award-winning productions as *The Making of the President 1960* (1963) and *The Rise and Fall of the Third Reich* (1968). Wolper is also credited with practically inventing the entertainment miniseries with *Sandburg's Lincoln, Roots* (1977), *Roots: The Next Generations* (1979), *The Thorn Birds* (1983), *North and South* (1984), and *Alex Haley's Queen* (1993). Wolper also produced the classic *Willie Wonka and the Chocolate Factory* (1971).